触动心灵的经典
— Heart-Touching Essay Series —

中英对照 · 双语典藏

U0735294

少年心事

励志篇

当拿云

Keeping Lofty Aspirations In Mind

希望这些散文能像一盏明灯，给你力量，让正在迷途中苦苦寻找出口的你坚定信念，看到人生的方向。

在这里/你能感受到心灵的自然表白
在这里/你能增强战胜命运的勇气与力量
在这里/你会发现成功其实并不遥远

丛书主编／戴艳萍 主编／刘晓琳 副主编／王宁

大连理工大学出版社

图书在版编目(CIP)数据

少年心事当拿云：励志篇：英汉对照 / 刘晓琳主编.
— 大连：大连理工大学出版社, 2012.8
（触动心灵的经典）
ISBN 978-7-5611-7192-9

Ⅰ.①少… Ⅱ.①刘… Ⅲ.①英语—汉语—对照读物
②散文集—世界 Ⅳ.①HN319.4:I

中国版本图书馆CIP数据核字(2012)第182778号

大连理工大学出版社出版
地址：大连市软件园路80号　　邮政编号：116023
发行：0411-84708842　邮购：04411-84703636　传真：0411-84701466
E-mail: dutp@dutp.cn　　DRL:http://www.dutp.cn
辽宁星海彩色印刷有限公司印刷　　大连理工大学出版社发行

幅面尺寸：168mm×235mm	印张：15	字数：233千
	印数：1~6000	
2012 年 8 月第 1 版		2012 年 8 月第 1 次印刷

责任编辑：李玉霞　　　　　　　　　　　　责任校对：蔡振兴
封面设计：王付青

ISBN 978-7-5611-7192-9　　　　　　　　　　定　价：25.00元

前言
preface

你改变不了环境，但你可以改变自己；

你改变不了事实，但你可以改变态度；

你改变不了过去，但你可以改变现在；

你不能控制他人，但你可以掌握自己；

你不能预知明天，但你可以把握今天；

你不可以样样顺利，但你可以事事尽心；

你不能延伸生命的长度，但你可以决定生命的宽度。

　　想首先与各位读者分享我读过的这一首短诗。自懂事起，我们就被父母、老师教育要有人生的志向，要有奋斗的目标，可是在我们寻梦的过程中，我们不断地受到环境的影响、外界的干扰、能力的限制等等，有时不得不向生命妥协，向命运低头，做着自己不喜欢的工作，在自我框架中被局限，想要逃离，却没有足够的勇气。最终，我们忘记了自己最初的梦想，浑浑噩噩地活着，只是憧憬着未来，却忘记了眼前最重要的事；只是一味地怨天尤人，却忘了要自己去成就梦想。难道我们真的要放弃吗？此刻我得请你作个决定，自我承诺今后绝不再自暴自弃，也绝不再自怜自哀。这并不是要你故意无视于所面对的困难，而是要你知道那种心态会阻止你拿出改变人生的行动。你要相信，纵使事情的发展有多悲观，我们都具有扭转的能力。别忘了，每个人都不免会碰上麻烦、问题、挫折或失望，我们怎样去面对，就注定会有什么样的人生。有时候决定你成败的不是外部环境，而是你自己对生命的态度。

　　即使受了伤，也不让泪水遮盖住了脸，把泪水擦干净，我们要重绽三月的笑颜。

　　即使迷了路，也不把忧伤刻在额前，星星总会升起来的，我们也总

会知道哪边是北、哪边是南。

我们不放弃，一天又一天，听风传递着雨的消息，听雨敲打湖的鼓面，那岁月的缆绳，终将成为我们抛向空中的闪电。

我们不放弃，一年又一年，看冰雪沉默在冬天响亮在春天，看春天把冰雪消融在大地的字里行间，那季节的色彩，终会被我们泼洒成斑斓的画卷。

在平凡的人生中，每个人都各自展示自己的精彩与光热，在生命的形式上，每一个不同的生命，就好像在同一个题目上，写下不同的内容而已。

在此，我们为各位读者精选了英美著名作家的有关励志修身题材的散文精品，这些作家将自己对人生的感悟承载于文字之中，他们用融合情趣、智慧、学问和亲身经历的文字与你推心置腹地交谈：马克·吐温会告诉你"不积跬步，无以至千里"的道理；戴尔·卡耐基让你脚踏实地，重视今天；威廉·里昂·费尔浦斯会告诉你什么才是生活的真谛；毛姆会教你宽以待人；奥格·曼迪诺会让你看到成功并不遥远；史蒂夫·乔布斯会让你觉得生活总是充满了未知数。只要坚持，你就不会倒下……从这些作品中我们可以感受到作者丰富的人生体验和对人生的彻悟，感受到智慧心灵的自然表白，增强战胜命运的勇气与力量。也许从他们的文章中，你会发现成功其实并不遥远，生活也并不可悲，只是有时我们自己迷失了方向，希望这些散文能像一盏明灯，给你力量，让正在迷途中苦苦寻找出口的你坚定信念，看到人生的方向。

最后，请大家记住下面的话：
活着，就是要寻找最棒的自己。
没有失败，只有暂时停止成功。

本册书主编为刘晓琳，副主编为王宁，参与本册书编写的还有：王婧、许剑楠、王星宇、王欣、王丽丽、余双全、周迈、汪露秋、项丹凤、王晓英、庄欣、孙礼中、刘瑜、宋沈黎、李雪等老师，在此表示感谢。

编　者
2012年8月

Contents 目录

目录

【 态度决定一切 】

【一叶知秋 脚踏实地】

【他山之石 可以攻玉】

目录

【锲而不舍　金石可镂】

目录

【及时当勉励　岁月不待人】

【不经一番寒彻骨　怎得梅花扑鼻香】

言近旨远
醍醐灌顶

Mark Twain

马克·吐温

马克·吐温（1835～1910），美国批判现实主义文学的奠基人，世界著名的短篇小说大师。他经历了美国从自由资本主义到帝国主义的发展过程，其思想和创作也表现为从轻快诙谐到辛辣讽刺再到悲观厌世的发展阶段。他的主要作品有短篇小说《汤姆·索亚历险记》（*The Adventures of Tom Sawyer*）、《竞选州长》（*Running for Governor, 1870*）、《哥尔斯密的朋友再度出洋》（*Goldsmith's Friend Abroad Again, 1870*）、长篇小说《哈克贝里·费恩历险记》（*The Adventures of Huckleberry Finn, 1884*）、《傻瓜威尔逊》（*The Tragedy of Pudd' nhead Wilson, 1894*）等，还有一些游记、杂文、政论，如《赤道环行记》（*Following the Equator, 1897*）等。

Advice to Youth

Being told I would be expected to talk here, I inquired what sort of talk I ought to make. They said it should be something suitable to youth — something didactic[1], instructive, or something in the nature of good advice. Very well, I have a few things in my mind which I have often longed to say for the instruction of the young; for it is in one's tender early years that such things will best take root and be most enduring and most valuable. First, then, I will say to you my young friends and I say it beseechingly[2], gurglingly[3] — always obey your parents, when they are present. This is the best policy in the long run, because if you don't, they will make you. Most parents think they know better than you do, and you can generally make more by humoring[4] that superstition than you can by acting on your own better judgment.

Be respectful to your superiors, if you have any, also to strangers, and sometimes to others. If a person offend you, and you are in doubt

忠告年轻人

被告知期望我在此谈一谈，我询问应该说什么话才合适。他们说我演讲的内容应该适合年轻人——教诲性的，具有教育意义的，或实质上属于忠告一类的话题。好吧，我脑中有一些想法，一直希望能表达出来，可以教育年轻人。因为正是在一个人品行尚未定型的时候，这些忠告才最容易扎根，影响才会最持久，也最有价值。那么，首先，我要对你们说，年轻人的朋友们，我要恳切地，迫切地说——在你们的父母在世时，要永远服从他们。从长远来看，这是上策，因为你们要是不服从的话，他们也会强迫你们服从。大多数父母认为他们比你们更了解世事。总的来说，顺应父母比坚持己见更有收获，尽管你们的判断可能更准确。

如果你们有上司的话，要尊敬他们，当然，还有那些陌生人，有时还有其他的一些

---

1 **didactic** /daɪ'dæktɪk/ *adj.* 教导的，说教的
2 **beseechingly** /bɪ'si:tʃɪŋli/ *adv.* 恳求地
3 **gurglingly** /'gɜːglɪŋli/ *adv.* 原意为水流的汩汩声，这里引申为"迫切地"
4 **humor** /'hju:mə(r)/ *v.* 顺应，迁就

as to[1] whether it was intentional or not, do not resort[2] to extreme measures; simply watch your chance and hit him with a brick. That will be sufficient. If you shall find that he had not intended any offense, come out frankly and confess[3] yourself in the wrong when you struck him; acknowledge it like a man and say you didn't mean to. Yes, always avoid violence; in this age of charity and kindliness, the time has gone by for such things. Leave dynamite[4] to the low and unrefined.

Go to bed early, get up early — this is wise. Some authorities say get up with the sun; some say get up with one thing, others with another. But a lark is really the best thing to get up with. It gives you a splendid reputation with everybody to know that you get up with the lark; and if you get the right kind of lark, and work at him right, you can easily train him to get up at half past nine, every time — no trick at all.

Now as to the matter of lying. You want to be very careful about lying; otherwise you are nearly sure to get caught. Once caught, you can never again be in the eyes to the good and the pure, what you were before. Many a young person[5] has injured himself permanently through a single clumsy and ill finished lie, the result of carelessness born of

人。如果有人冒犯了你们，而你们又搞不清楚他是不是故意的，不要采取极端的措施；只需等待时机，用砖头砸他一下就够了。如果你们发现他并非有意冒犯，那么你坦诚地承认自己打他是不应该的，要做得像个男子汉，并说明不是故意的。是的，永远要避免使用暴力；处在这个仁慈、谦和的年代，为这种事情计较的年代已经过去了。让身份低贱、没教养的人去动手动脚吧。

早睡早起——这是明智之举。有些权威人士说与日同起，有些人说与这种事物同起，有些人说与那种事物同起。但是百灵鸟真的是最佳的同起之物。所有人知道你伴着百灵鸟起床，你会因此名声远扬；如果你弄到合适的百灵鸟，用正确的方法加以调教，那么可以轻易地训练它在九点半起床，每次都是——绝不骗你。

现在我们说说撒谎的问题。要想撒谎的话，你们就要格外小心，否则你们肯定会被揭穿。而一旦被揭穿，在品行端

---

1 as to 关于
2 resort /rɪˈzɔːt/ v. 求助，凭借，该词常与介词to连用
3 confess /kənˈfes/ v. 供认，承认；坦白
4 dynamite /ˈdaɪnəmaɪt/ n. 炸药；充满火药味的东西
5 many a young person 相当于many persons，但many a person的谓语动词应用单数形式

incomplete training. Some authorities hold that the young ought not to lie at all. That of course, is putting it rather stronger than necessary; still while I cannot go quite so far as that, I do maintain, and I believe I am right, that the young ought to be temperate in the use of this great art until practice and experience shall give them that confidence, elegance, and precision which alone can make the accomplishment graceful and profitable. Patience, diligence, painstaking[1] attention to — these are requirements; these in time, will make the student perfect; upon these only, may he rely as the sure foundation for future eminence. Think what tedious years of study, thought, practice, experience, went to the equipment of that peerless old master who was able to impose upon[2] the whole world the lofty and sounding maxim that "Truth is mighty and will prevail" — the most majestic compound fracture of fact which any of woman born has yet achieved. For the history of our race, and each individual experience, are sewn thick with evidences that a truth is not hard to kill, and that a lie well told is immortal. There is in Boston a monument of the man who discovered anesthesia[3]; many people are aware, in these latter days, that that man didn't discover it

---

1　painstaking /'peɪnzteɪkɪŋ/　*adj.* 费尽心思的，非常小心的
2　impose upon　强加于
3　anesthesia /ˌænɪs'θiːzɪə/　*n.* 麻木

正、心灵纯洁的人眼里，你们就再也不是从前的你们了。许多年轻人往往因为一个漏洞百出的谎言而给自己带来终身的伤害，这种疏忽大意往往是由于不完整的教育而导致的。有些权威人士认为年轻人压根儿就不应该撒谎。当然，这也未免太绝对了；虽然我不会这样说，但我坚持认为，而且我也相信我是对的，即年轻人不应过分地运用这门伟大的艺术，特别是在他们没有足够的训练和经验使他们能够充满自信、风度优雅并言辞精确之前，因为具备这三点才能在撒谎时不伤大雅，带来益处。耐心、勤奋、小心谨慎地对待细枝末节——这些都是必备的条件；这些也迟早会把学生造就成一个完人；只有这些品质，才是他将来可能赖以成名的坚实基础。想想那位举世无双的大师，他经历了多少年枯燥乏味的学习、思考、训练和体验，才能迫使全世界接受"真理是强大的而且终将取胜"这句崇高而掷地有声的格言——这是关于事实的复杂层面道出的最豪迈的话语，迄今任何出自娘胎的人都未曾获得。因为，无论是在人类这一物种的历史上，还是在个人的经历中都有许多事实表明，真理很容易被扼杀，而高明的谎言

at all, but stole the discovery from another man. Is this truth mighty, and will it prevail? Ah no, my hearers, the monument is made of hardy material, but the lie it tells will outlast it a million years. An awkward, feeble, leaky lie is a thing which you ought to make it your unceasing study to avoid; such a lie as that has no more real permanence than an average truth. Why, you might as well tell the truth at once and be done with it. A feeble, stupid, preposterous[1] lie will not live two years except it be a slander[2] upon somebody. It is indestructible, then of course, but that is no merit of yours. A final word: begin your practice of this gracious and beautiful art early begin now. If I had begun earlier, I could have learned how[3].

Never handle firearms carelessly. The sorrow and suffering that have been caused through the innocent but heedless handling of firearms by the young! Only four days ago, right in the next farm house to the one where I am spending the summer, a grandmother, old and gray and sweet, one of the loveliest spirits in the land, was sitting at her work, when her young grandson crept in and got down an old, battered, rusty gun which had not been touched for many years and was supposed not

却可以永生。在波士顿矗立着一座纪念麻醉剂发明者的雕像，许多人后来才发现，雕像上的人根本就没有发明什么麻醉剂，他只是从别人那儿偷来了这项发明。在这里，真理还是全能的吗？真理还能战胜一切吗？哦，不！听众们，虽然这座雕像是用坚固耐久的材料制成的，但它所描述的谎言会比它本身多流传百万年。你们仍需不断地学习，以避免那些拙劣的、站不住脚的、有破绽的谎言，因为这样的谎言与普通的事实一样不会真正永恒地流传下来。为什么呢？因为普通的事实你们可以一下子就讲出来。一个站不住脚的、愚蠢的、荒谬的谎言不会流传两年以上——除非是对某人的诽谤。当然，这种谎言是不会被戳穿的，但是这样做是不道德的。最后，我需要说明的是：趁早学习这门高雅而又美丽的艺术——现在就开始。要是我早点开始学习的话，现在早就掌握其中的奥妙了。

玩弄火器时，切忌粗心大意。虽然年轻人并无恶意，然而不加小心地玩弄火器曾造成过多么大的悲伤与痛苦啊！就在四天前，在我避暑的农舍隔壁家，一位花白头发、和蔼可亲的老太太（也是当地最受人喜爱的人物之一），正坐在那儿干活儿，

1 **preposterous** /prɪˈpɒstərəs/ *adj.* 荒谬的
2 **slander** /ˈslɑːndə(r)/ *n.* 诽谤，诋毁
3 本句是 if 条件句的虚拟语气，表示该事件没有发生过，只是说话人的一种愿望

言近旨远 醍醐灌顶

to be loaded, and pointed it at her, laughing and threatening to shoot. In her fright she ran screaming and pleading toward the door on the other side of the room; but as she passed him he placed the gun almost against her very breast and pulled the trigger! He had supposed it was not loaded. And he was right it wasn't. So there wasn't any harm done. It is the only case of that kind I ever heard of. Therefore, just the same, don't you meddle with[1] old unloaded firearms; they are the most deadly and unerring hinges that have ever been created by man. You don't have to take any pains at all with them; you don't have to have a rest, you don't have to have any sights on the gun, you don't have to take aim, even. No, you just pick out a relative and bang away, and you are sure to get him. A youth who cannot hit a cathedral at thirty yards with a Gating gun in three quarters of an hour, can take up an old empty musket and bag his grandmother every time, at a hundred. Think what Waterloo would have been if one of the armies had been boys armed with old muskets[2] supposed not to be loaded, and the other army had been composed of their female relations. The very thought of it make one shudder.

There are many sorts of books; but good ones are the sort for the young to read.

1 meddle with 干预
2 musket /ˈmʌskɪt/ n. 火枪

这时，她的小孙子偷偷地溜了进来，拿着一枝老式的、破损的、锈迹斑斑的枪———一把多年没人动过的枪，想必也没有装子弹。小孙子用枪指着她，哈哈笑着吓唬说要开枪。惊恐之余，老太太尖叫着朝房间对面的门跑去，一边跑，一边央求他不要开枪。可是，当她跑过他身前时，他还是把枪几乎顶在她的胸口上，并扣动了扳机！他认为枪里根本不会有子弹。当然，他是对的——枪里的确没有装子弹。因此也没有造成什么真正的伤害。但是，这是我听说过的此类事件中唯一没有造成任何伤亡的事件。因此，不要摆弄那些老式破旧的、没装子弹的火器，它们是人类制造出来的最致命的，但又是最准确无误的家伙。有了它们，你们大可不必忧愁，你们不用花什么工夫，枪上也不用安装瞄准器，甚至也不用瞄准。是的，你们只需要挑个亲戚，然后，对着他，扣动扳机，准能击中他。一个年轻人站在30尺开外端着加特林多管机枪扫射三刻钟也打不中教堂，但站在100尺外，用一枝旧式的、空膛的火枪，他可以准确地射中他的祖母，而且百发百中。想想看，如果滑铁卢战役的交战双方，一方由端着没装弹药的火枪的男孩组成，另一方则由他们的女亲戚们组成。结果会

Remember that. They are a great, an inestimable and unspeakable means of improvement. Therefore be careful in your selection, my young friends; be very careful; confine yourselves exclusively to Robertson's Sermons[1], Baxter's Saint's Rest[2], The Innocents Abroad[3], and works of that kind.

But I have said enough. I hope you will treasure up the instructions which I have given you, and make them a guide to your feet and a light to your understanding. Build your character thoughtfully and painstakingly upon these precepts, and by and by, when you have got it built, you will be surprised and gratified to see how nicely and sharply it resembles everybody else.

怎么样呢，一想到这种情景人们就会不寒而栗。

世界上有许多种书籍，但最好的是给年轻人读的那种。请记住，它们对人类的自我完善起着巨大的、无法用语言描述的作用。因此，我的青年朋友们，你们给自己选书时，一定要小心，而且要非常小心，尽量阅读罗伯逊的《讲道集》，巴科斯特的《圣徒的安息》，《傻子出国记》这类图书。

我已经说得够多的了。我希望你们能够珍惜我给你们的这些教诲，把它们作为你们行动的指南和理智的灯塔。当你们培养自己的性格的时候，应该认真思考、细心琢磨这些忠告。当你们的性格慢慢形成之后，你们就会惊喜地意识到，你们的品质跟其他人的品质有着如此明显的相似之处。

1 Sermons《讲道集》 (Sermons Preached at Trinity Chapel Brighton I~V, 1855~1890)，为英国神学家、社会改革者弗雷德里克·威廉·罗伯逊 (Frederick William Robertson, 1816~1853) 所著
2 Saint's Rest《圣徒的安息》 (1650)，为英国基德敏斯特 (Kiddermi-nster) 长老会牧师理查德·巴科斯特 (Richard Baxter, 1615~1691) 的宗教经典之作，其被誉为"清教徒之父"
3 The Innocents Abroad《傻子出国记》，为马克·吐温于1869年所写的旅欧报道，讲述一个美国游客在欧陆和中东的所见所闻，虽所到之处尽皆著名博物馆或圣地，但叙述者抛开崇拜之心，直抒己见，且不乏幽默和调侃。

含英咀华

细细品读本文，作者并没有如其他大师一样用激昂的文字来激励年轻人，只是一如既往地用诙谐幽默的语言写了一些生活的琐事，如：要尊敬长辈，早睡早起，要诚实守信，不要有暴力倾向，要热爱读书等，而这些看似不起眼的，被大家所忽视的事情，却是塑造一个有作为的年轻人最基本的条件。所以如果你是一个涉世之初的年轻人，就要好好读读本文，社会喧嚣复杂，要学会拒绝虚假、肤浅、空想和庸碌。

Philip Dormer Stanhope

菲利普·道摩·斯坦霍普

菲利普·道摩·斯坦霍普（1694～1773），即切斯菲尔德勋爵，英国著名的政治家，外交家兼作家，曾任驻荷兰大使、国务大臣等。他风流倜傥，在英国是讲究礼仪的典范，以著作《给儿子的信》而闻名于世。

Letter to His Son

Dear boy,

The art of pleasing is a very necessary one to possess, but a very difficult one to acquire. It can hardly be reduced to rules; and your own good sense and observation will teach you more of it than I can. "Do as you would be done by," is the surest method that I know of pleasing. Observe carefully what pleases you in others, and probably the same things in you will please others. If you are pleased with the complaisance[1] and attention of others to your humors, your tastes, or your weaknesses, depend on it, the same complaisance and attention on your part to theirs will equally please them. Take the tone of the company that you are in, and do not pretend to give it; be serious, gay, or even trifling, as you find the present humor of the company; this is an attention due from every individual to the majority. Do not tell stories in company; there is nothing more tedious and disagreeable; if by chance you know a very short story, and exceedingly applicable to the present subject of conversation, tell it in as few words as possible; and even then, throw out that you do not love to tell stories, but that the shortness of it

给儿子的一封信

亲爱的孩子：

惹人喜欢是一门甚有必要然而又不易学到的艺术，很难将其归纳成规则。你自己良好的判断力与观察力将使你领悟到比我教授给你的还要多的东西。"己所不欲，勿施于人"，据我所知，这是取悦于人的最可靠的办法。细心留意别人怎样做让你愉快，那么很可能你做同样的事也会使别人愉悦。如果别人对你的性情、兴趣甚至弱点甚为关心，让你满心欢喜，请相信，你对别人施以同样的热情和关照，也一定会使他们高兴。与人为伴来往时，需顺应其中的氛围，勿娇揉造作，根据同伴的心境一起庄重严肃，或开怀一乐甚至调笑一番，这是每个人对群体应具备的态度。在人前不要长篇大论，没有事情比这更冗长乏味和令人不悦了。如果你恰好有一则很简短而又相当切题的故事，可用最简洁明了的语言叙述一番。即便如此，也要

---

1 complaisance /kəmˈpleɪzəns/ *n.* 彬彬有礼

tempted you.

Of all the things banish the egotism[1] out of your conversation, and never think of entertaining people with your own personal concerns or private affairs; though they are interesting to you, they are tedious and impertinent[2] to everybody else; besides that, one cannot keep one's own private affairs to secret. Whatever you think your own excellencies may be, do not affectedly display them in company; nor labor, as many people do, to give that turn to the conversation, which may supply you with an opportunity of exhibiting them. If they are real, they will infallibly[3] be discovered, without your pointing them out yourself, and with much more advantage. Never maintain an argument with heat and clamor, though you think to know yourself to be in the right; but give your opinion modestly and coolly, which is the only way to convince; and, if that does not do, try to change the conversation, by saying, with good humor, "We shall hardly convince one another; nor is it necessary that we should, so let us talk of something else."

Remember that there is a local propriety to be observed in all companies; and that what is extremely proper in one company may be, and often is, highly improper in another. The

表示出你不擅长讲述，而仅是因为它太简短才使你情不自禁那样做。

在交谈中，首先要摈弃以自我为中心的癖好，绝不要试图让别人对自己的私事或者自己关注的事产生兴趣。尽管这些事情对于你来说趣味横生，但对于别人却味同嚼蜡，不得要领。再者，个人的私事也不可能永远隐秘。无论你自以为有什么长处，切忌在人前自爱自怜地展示，也不要像许多人那样，挖空心思地引导谈话，以伺机自我表现一番。如果你确有长处，必会被别人发现，不必自己点出，何况这样做最好。当与人有是非之争时，绝不要激动地大喊大叫，即使你自以为正确，也要冷静地说出自己的意见，这是说服人的唯一方法。但如果这样仍不奏效，就试着变个话题，高高兴兴地说："我俩谁也说服不了谁，而且也不是非得说服对方不可，我们讨论别的吧。"

要记住，与人交往时要尊重习俗的礼仪。在这一群人中恰

---

1 **egotism** /'egətɪzəm/ *n.* 自大，自负
2 **impertinent** /ɪm'pɜːtɪnənt/ *adj.* 鲁莽的，无礼的
3 **infallibly** /ɪn'fæləbli/ *adv.* 绝对无误地

言近旨远 醍醐灌顶

jokes, the bon-mots[1], the little adventures, which may do very well in one company, will seem flat and tedious, when related in another. The particular characters, the habit, the cant[2] of one company may give merit to a word, or a gesture, which would have none at all if divested[3] of those accidental circumstances. Here people very commonly err; and fond of something that has entertained them in one company, and in certain circumstances, repeat it with emphasis in another, where it is either insipid[4], or, it may be, offensive, by being ill-timed or misplaced. Nay, they often do it with this silly preamble[5]: "I will tell you an excellent thing," or, "I will tell you the best thing in the world." This raises expectations, which, when absolutely disappointed, make the relator of this excellent thing look, very deservedly, like a fool.

If you would particularly gain the affection and friendship of particular people, whether men or women, endeavor to find out their predominant excellency, if they have one, and their prevailing weakness, which everybody has; and do justice to the one, and something more than justice to the other. Men have various objects in which they may excel, or at least would be thought to excel; and, though they love to hear justice done to

如其分的话语，对另一群人而言却经常不适宜。对某些人适宜的幽默、妙语、甚至小小的出格行为，换个地方会显得平淡乏味。说一个词儿或打一个手势，在某一群人中即暗示着某种性格、习惯和隐语，而一旦离开那种特定氛围，就会毫无意义。人们常在这一点上犯错。他们喜欢把在某群人、某种环境中的得意言行随便搬到别的地方使用，而此时却风趣尽失，或不合时宜，或张冠李戴而唐突无聊。是的，他们经常用这样笨拙的开场白："告诉你一件很棒的事！"或者"我要告诉你世界上最精彩的事"。这些话能勾起对方的期待，可对方一旦彻底失望，说这些话的人看起来就像个十足的傻子。

如果你想获得别人的好感和友情，无论是男人或女人，要特别留意去发现他们可能具备的长处，以及他们明显的不足之处。当然人人都会有缺陷，要公正地评价别人的长处，却要给别人的弱点更多的宽容。人们还会有许多过人之处，或者至少具有可以看做优秀

---

1 bon-mot *n.* 妙语
2 cant /kant/ *n.* 行话，隐语
3 divest /daɪ'vest/ *v.* 使摆脱，使脱去，夺去
4 insipid /ɪn'sɪpɪd/ *adj.* 乏味的，枯燥的
5 preamble /priː'æmbl/ *n.* 前文，序文

them, where they know that they excel, yet they are most and best flattered upon those points where they wish to excel, and yet are doubtful whether they do or not.

的地方。尽管人们喜欢听到对其自知的优点的赞美，但他们最感兴趣的乃是对自己渴望具备且尚不自信的长处的赞许。

含英咀华

　　这是一封在西方社会广为流传的信，表达父亲对孩子恳切的叮咛与教诲。在文章中，父亲教导孩子如何讨人喜欢，如何与人交流，如何对待好感和友情，文字朴实无华，字里行间充满了一个父亲对孩子的殷切嘱托和拳拳父爱。父辈们的建议，虽然不能避免我们在人生的路上摔跤，却至少能拉住我们，使我们不至于落入悬崖，掉进深渊，使我们不至于重蹈父辈们的旧辙。文章句句有力，字字精辟，入情入理，充满了真知灼见。

Barbara Pierce Bush
芭芭拉·皮尔斯·布什

芭芭拉·皮尔斯·布什（1925～），美国前总统乔治·赫伯特·沃克·布什（George Herbert Walker Bush，1924～）的夫人，前任总统小布什的母亲。芭芭拉在丈夫的政治生涯中一直扮演重要的角色，她友善及直率的性格使其深得人心。芭芭拉深受美国人民的爱戴，被誉为"大众的祖母"。她的白发，她的慈祥，她的热心给人一种温暖、和蔼可亲的感觉。在作为总统夫人期间，她致力于建立一个更有文化的美国，并积极投身于慈善事业。

Commencement Address at Wellesley College[1] (Excerpts)

卫尔斯利学院毕业典礼上的讲话（节选）

More than ten years ago, when I was invited here to talk about our experiences in the People's Republic of China, I was struck by both the natural beauty of your campus and the spirit of this place.

Wellesley, you see, is not just a place but an idea — an experiment in excellence in which diversity is not just tolerated, but is embraced[2]. The essence of this spirit was captured in a moving speech about tolerance given last year by a student body president of one of your sister colleges. She related the story by Robert Fulghum[3] about a young pastor, finding himself in charge of some very energetic children, hits upon a game called "Giants, Wizards, and Dwarfs." "You have to decide now," the pastor instructed the children, "which you are — a giant, a wizard or a dwarf?" At that, a small girl tugging at his pants leg, asked, "But where do the mermaids[4] stand?" And the pastor tells her there are no mermaids. And she says, "Oh yes there are. I am a mermaid."

十多年前，我被邀请来这里介绍我们在中国的经历时，你们校园的自然美景和这里的精神就已经给我留下了深刻的印象。

卫尔斯利不仅是一个地方，而且代表了一种思想——追求卓越，不仅包容而且拥护多样性。去年，你们一个姐妹学院的学生会主席在一场令人感动的关于包容的演讲中，充分体现了这种精神的精髓。她叙述了由罗伯特·富尔格姆写的关于一个年轻牧师的故事。牧师负责照看一群活泼的小孩，于是想到带他们玩一种叫"巨人、男巫和小矮人"的游戏，牧师告诉孩子们："你们现在就得做决定，你是哪一种人——巨人，男巫还是小矮人？"这时，一个小女孩用力拉他的裤腿，问道："但是美人鱼站在哪儿？"牧师告诉她没有美人鱼，她说，"噢，不，有的，我就是美人鱼。"

1 该学院是世界上最著名的私立文科女校，以为美国总统和社会名流培养了最多的第一夫人而著称
2 embrace /ɪmˈbreɪs/ v. 欣然接受，乐意采纳
3 Robert Fulghum 罗伯特·富尔格姆（1937—），美国当代作家、哲学家
4 mermaid /ˈmɜːmeɪd/ n. 美人鱼

Commencement Address at Wellesley College 1(Excerpts)

Now this little girl knew what she was, and she was not about to give up on either her identity, or the game. She intended to take her place wherever mermaids fit into the scheme of things. Where do the mermaids stand? All of those who are different, those who do not fit the boxes and the pigeonholes? "Answer that question," wrote Fulghum, "And you can build a school, a nation, or a whole world." As that very wise young woman said, "Diversity, like anything worth having, requires effort. Effort to learn about and respect difference, to be compassionate[1] with one another, to cherish our own identity, and to accept unconditionally the same in others."

You should all be very proud that this is the Wellesley spirit. Now I know your first choice today was Alice Walker[2] — guess how I know! — known for The Color Purple. Instead you got me — known for — the color of my hair! Alice Walker's book has a special resonance[3] here. At Wellesley, each class is known by a special color. For four years the Class of 90 has worn the color purple. Today you meet on Severance Green to say goodbye to all of that, to begin a new and very personal journey, to search for your own true colors.

1 compassionate /kəmˈpæʃənət/　adj.　有同情心的
2 Alice Walker　爱丽斯·沃克（1944—），美国当代黑人女作家，其长篇小说紫色》(The Color Purple, 1982)曾获得普利策奖和美国国家图书奖
3 resonance /ˈrezənəns/　n.　共鸣

这个小女孩知道她想要什么，她既不想放弃她的身份，也不想退出这个游戏。不管美人鱼在游戏中适合安排在哪个位置，她只愿扮演这个角色。美人鱼站在哪儿？所有不适合常规定位、不适合传统类别的人站在哪儿呢？"回答这个问题，"福尔格姆写道，"你就能建立一所学校，一个国家，或整个世界。"正如那位非常聪明的年轻女士说的，"就像任何值得拥有的东西一样，多样性需要人们努力。努力去学习并尊重差异，与人为善，珍惜我们自己的身份，并且无条件接受他人身上不一样的东西。"

你们应为此而感到骄傲，这就是卫尔斯利精神。我知道今天你们欢迎的人选是爱丽丝·沃克——猜猜看我是怎么知道的！——是从《紫色》这本书中知道的。然而你们却把我找来了——因为我的头发的颜色特别吧。爱丽丝·沃克的书在这儿有特殊的共鸣。在卫尔斯利，每个年级都有一个特殊的颜色，四年来，90届的全体学生一直都佩戴紫色。今天你们聚集在锡瓦伦斯·格林，告别这所有的一切，开始一次全新的个人旅程，去寻求真正属于你自己的颜色。

In the world that awaits you, beyond the shores of Lake Waban, no one can say what your true colors will be. But this I do know: You have a first class education from a first class school. And so you need not, probably cannot, live a "paint-by-numbers[1]" life. Decisions are not irrevocable[2]. Choices do come back. And as you set off from Wellesley, I hope that many of you will consider making three very special choices.

The first is to believe in something larger than yourself, to get involved in some of the big ideas of our time. I chose literacy because I honestly believe that if more people could read, write and comprehend, we would be that much closer to solving so many of the problems that plague[3] our nation and our society.

And early on I made another choice which I hope you'll make as well. Whether you are talking about education, career, or service, you're talking about life — and life really must have joy. It's supposed to be fun!

One of the reasons I made the most important decision of my life, to marry George Bush, is because he made me laugh. It's true, sometimes we've laughed through our tears. But that shared laughter has been one of our strongest bonds. Find the joy in life, because as

在等待你的世界里，告别了沃本湖畔，没有人可以说出你的真正颜色将是什么。但是有一点我是知道的：你们在一个一流的学校接受了一流的教育。所以你不需要、或许也不能够过一种循规蹈矩的生活。决定不是无法挽回，选择也会重新再来。当你们从卫尔斯利出发时，我希望你们中的许多人考虑三个特别的选择。

第一种选择，信仰某些比你自身更为博大的东西，并参与到我们这个时代一些大的构想之中。我选择教育是因为我坚信如果更多的人能读会写并且善于理解，那么我们会更好地沟通以解决困扰我们国家和社会的许多问题。

早期，我做过另一种选择，希望你们也选择这个。无论你们是在谈论教育、事业还是服务，你们都是在谈论生活——生活必须要有快乐，生活也应该是充满乐趣的。

我一生中做的最重要的决定是与乔治·布什结婚，其原因之一是因为他使我开心，真的，有时我们会喜极而泣。那种分享的笑声是我们之间最强大的黏合剂之一。发现生活中的快乐，因为正如菲利斯·布

---

1 **paint-by-numbers** 循规蹈矩的生活
2 **irrevocable** /ɪˈrevəkəbl/ *adj.* 不能唤回的，不能取消的，不能变更的
3 **plague** /pleɪg/ *v.* 折磨，使……苦恼

卫尔斯利学院毕业典礼上的讲话（节选）
Commencement Address at Wellesley College 1(Excerpts)

Ferris Bueller said on his day off[1], "Life moves pretty fast; and ya don't stop and look around once in a while, ya gonna miss it!"

The third choice that must not be missed is to cherish your human connections: your relationships with family and friends. For several years, you've had impressed upon you the importance to your career of dedication and hard work. And, of course, that's true. But as important as your obligations as a doctor, a lawyer, a business leader will be, you are a human being first. And those human connections — with spouses, with children, with friends — are the most important investments you will ever make.

At the end of your life, you will never regret not having passed one more test, winning one more verdict[2], or not closing one more deal. You will regret time not spent with a husband, a child, a friend or a parent.

勒在影片《春天不是读书天》中所说："生活节奏很快，如果你不停下来欣赏一下，那么你会错过很多风景。"

第三种不应错过的选择是珍惜你的人际关系：你与家庭和朋友的关系。因为几年来，你们已经对奉献事业和努力工作的重要性有了深刻的印象，当然那是真的。与你作为医生、律师或企业领导人的职责同等重要的是你首先是一个人。人与人的关系——配偶、子女和朋友——是你最重要的投资。

在你生命的尽头，你不会后悔没有通过某次考试，没有赢得某个案子，或者没有做成某笔生意，而会为没有花时间陪伴丈夫、孩子、朋友或父母感到遗憾。

---

1 Ferris Bueller said on his day off: Ferris Bueller's Day Off（《春天不是读书天》）是一部1986年由John Hughes 执导的喜剧电影，片中主角为一名叫菲利斯·布勒的高三学生
2 verdict /ˈvɜːdɪkt/　n.　判决

含英咀华

　　本文是1990年芭芭拉接受卫尔斯利学院的邀请在该校的毕业典礼上的发言。当时这一举动遭到该学院150名即将毕业学生的抗议。抗议者认为芭芭拉并无任何建树，只是嫁给了一位有名的丈夫而已。但抗议却为芭芭拉赢得了男女平等主义者的同情和支持，他们认为芭芭拉所选择的是一条属于她自己、也适合她自己的人生道路，卫尔斯利学院的邀请是对女性选择权的尊重。在本文中，作者首先告诉即将毕业的年轻人，不论何时何地，不要轻易改变自己，要坚持本色，但同时也要学会求同存异，然后作者又给年轻人提出三条忠告，在追求事业成功的同时，不要抛弃信仰，不要忘记快乐地生活和善待你周围的人。

William Faulkner
威廉·福克纳

威廉·福克纳 (1897~1962)二十世纪美国最重要的作家之一，美国"南方文学"派的创始人，也是整个西方最有影响的现代派小说家之一。他最著名的作品有：《喧哗与骚动》（*The Sound and the Fury, 1929*）、《我弥留之际》（*As I Lay Dying , 1930*）、《八月之光》（*Light in August , 1932*）、《押沙龙，押沙龙！》（*Absalom, Absalom! , 1937*）等。他还是多产的短篇小说家，主要有：《献给爱米丽的玫瑰》（*A Rose for Emily, 1930*）、《干燥的九月》（*Dry September, 1931*）等。1949年作品《我弥留之际》获诺贝尔奖，他作品最大的外在特点是绵延婉转、结构极为繁复的长句子和反复斟酌推敲后选取的精巧词汇，并且大量运用意识流、多角度叙述和陈述中时间推移等富有创新性的文学手法。

The Spirit of Man

I feel that this award was not made to me as a man, but to my work — a life's work in the agony and sweat of the human spirit, not for glory and least of all for profit, but to create out of the materials of the human spirit something which did not exist before. So this award is only mine in trust. It will not be difficult to find a dedication[1] for the money part of it commensurate[2] with the purpose and significance of its origin. But I would like to do the same with the acclaim[3] too, by using this moment as a pinnacle from which I might be listened to by the young men and women already dedicated to the same anguish and travail[4], among whom is already that one who will some day stand here where I am standing.

Our tragedy today is a general and universal physical fear so long sustained[5] by now that we can even bear it. There are no longer problems of the spirit. There is only the question: When will I be blown up? Because of this, the young man or woman writing today has forgotten the problems of the human heart in conflict with itself which

人类的精神

我觉得诺贝尔奖并非授予我个人，而是授予我的工作——一项艰辛而痛苦的毕生投入的人类精神的工作，它无关荣耀，更无关金钱，而是要创造人类精神世界中前所未有的东西。所以，这个奖只是对我的信任。尽管我们不难发现这个奖项在金钱方面作出的充分贡献、体现了创始的目的和意义，但我仍然要和这些掌声和喝彩一道，把这个时刻作为一个高台，让那些有志献身于同样的痛苦和辛劳的年轻人听到我的声音；在他们当中，某天必定会有人站在我站的地方。

我们今天的悲剧是人们普遍存在一种生理上的恐惧，这种恐惧存在已久，以致我们已经习惯了。现在已经不存在精神上的问题了，唯一的问题是：我什么时候会被炸得粉身

---

1 dedication /ˌdedɪˈkeɪʃn/   *n.*   献词
2 commensurate /kəˈmenʃərət/   *adj.*   同样大小的，相称的
3 acclaim /əˈkleɪm/   *n.*   喝彩，欢呼，赞同
4 travail /ˈtræveɪl/   *n.*   辛劳
5 sustained /səˈsteɪn/   *v.*   维持；使保持

alone can make good writing because only that is worth writing about, worth the agony and the sweat.

He must learn them again. He must teach himself that the basest of all things is to be afraid; and, teaching himself that, forget it forever, leaving no room in his workshop for anything but the old verities[1] and truths of the heart, the old universal truths lacking which any story is ephemeral[2] and doomed — love and honor and pity and pride and compassion and sacrifice. Until he does so, he labors under a curse. He writes not of love but of lust, of defeats in which nobody loses anything of value, of victories without hope and, worst of all, without pity or compassion. His grieves grieve on no universal bones, leaving no scars. He writes not of the heart but of the glands.

Until he relearns these things, he will write as though he stood among and watched the end of man. I decline to accept the end of man. It is easy enough to say that man is immortal simply because he will endure: that when the last ding-dong of doom has clanged and faded from the last worthless rock hanging tideless in the last red and dying evening, that even then there will still be one more sound: that of his puny inexhaustible voice, still talking. I refuse to accept this. I believe that man will not

碎骨？正因如此，今天从事写作的男女青年已经忘记了人类内心的冲突。然而，只有接触到这种内心冲突才能产生出好作品，因为这是唯一值得写、值得付出心血去经营的题材。

人们必须重温这些，必须教会自己：世间最可鄙的事情莫过于恐惧；他必须使自己永远忘却恐惧，在自己的工作室里只为亘古不变的心灵的真理留出位置。因为离开这些亘古不变的真理，任何小说都会如蜉蝣朝菌一般的短命——不论爱或荣誉或怜悯或自豪或同情或牺牲。如果不这样做，他的一切劳作都会受到诅咒。他所描绘的不是爱情而是肉欲，他所记述的失败里不会有人失去任何有价值的东西，他所描绘的胜利中也没有希望，最糟糕的是，没有同情和怜悯。他的悲哀缺乏普遍性的深度，只是轻描淡写而已。他所描述的不是人类的心灵，而是人类的内分泌物。

只有当他重温了这些，他写作起来才会如同亲临其境，如同亲历人的结局。我不

---

1 verity /ˈverəti/ *n.* 真理
2 ephemeral /ɪˈfemərəl/ *adj.* 朝生暮死的，生命短暂的

merely endure: he will prevail. He is immortal, not because he alone among creatures has an inexhaustible voice, but because he has a soul, a spirit capable of[1] compassion and sacrifice and endurance.

The poet's, the writer's duty is to write about these things. It is his privilege[2] to help man endure by lifting his heart, by reminding him of the courage and honor and hope and pride and compassion and pity and sacrifice which have been the glory of his past. The poet's voice need not merely be the record of man, it can be one of the props, the pillars to help him endure and prevail.

属于接受人的终结。谁都可以脱口说出：人是不朽的，就因为他可以忍耐；在夜幕时分，即便临终的钟声在残阳映照的最后一块荒芜的枯石上响过、消逝，仍将还有一个声音：他的声音仍在叙述，微弱而不绝如缕。我拒绝接受这些。我相信，人不仅仅能够忍耐，他还能够超越。他之所以不朽，不是因为在芸芸众生中唯独他可以发出不绝如缕的声音，而在于他有灵魂，能够承载同情、牺牲和忍受的灵魂。

而诗人和作家的责任就是描写这些事情。诗人和作家的特权就是帮助一个人升华心灵，学会忍耐；就是唤醒他的勇气，他的荣誉，他的希望，他的自豪，他的同情心，他的牺牲精神。这些都是他往日的荣光。诗人的声音不仅仅是人类的简单记录，而且还是能够帮助人类持续和获胜的支柱之一。

---

1 capable of　有能力。例如：Only human beings are capable of speech.（只有人类具有说话的能力。）
2 privilege /ˈprɪvəlɪdʒ/　n. 特权

含英咀华

　　本文是福克纳在1949年于斯德哥尔摩发表的诺贝尔文学奖得奖感言，文中勉励作家必须提升自己的心灵，时时以爱、怜悯和牺牲来唤醒人类亘古的真理，只有这样，作家才能写出长久流传的优秀作品。在本演讲中，我们可以看到作者关于好作品的标准：只有接触到人的内心冲突才能产生出好作品。这对梦想成为作家的人极有启发。同时，在这席发言中，我们可以体会到一代伟大作家的性格。

Bertrand Russell
伯特兰·罗素

伯特兰·罗素(1872~1970)英国哲学家、数学家、社会学家，也是上世纪西方最著名、影响最大的学者和社会活动家，并于1950年获得诺贝尔学奖。其主要著作有《意义与真理的探究》(*An Inquiry into Meaning and Truth, 1940*)、《人类知识的范围和局限》(*Human Knowledge: Its Scope and Limits, 1948*)、《数学原理》(*The Principles of Mathematics, 1903*)等。罗素学识渊博，通晓的学科之多大概是二十世纪学者们少有的。而且，他在哲学、数学、教育学、社会学、政治学等许多领域都颇有建树。他的哲学观点多变，以善于吸取别人见解、勇于指出自己的错误和弱点而著称。早期属于新实在主义，晚年逐渐转向逻辑实证主义。

言近旨远 醍醐灌顶

Three Passions

Three passions, simple but overwhelmingly[1] strong, have governed my life: the longing for love, the search for knowledge, and unbearable pity for the suffering of mankind. These passions, like great winds, have blown me hither and thither[2], in a way ward course over a deep ocean of anguish[3], reaching to the very verge[4] of despair.

I have sought love, first, because it brings ecstasy[5] — ecstasy so great that I would often have sacrificed all the rest of my life for a few hours for this joy. I have sought it, next, because it relieves loneliness — that terrible loneliness in which one shivering consciousness looks over the rim of the world into the cold unfathomable[6] lifeless abyss. I have sought it, finally, because in the union of love I have seen, in a mystic miniature, the prefiguring[7] vision of the heaven that saints and poets have imagined. This is what I sought, and though it might seem too good for human life, this is what — at last — I have found.

With equal passion I have sought knowl-

---

1 overwhelmingly /ˌəʊvə'welmɪŋli/   *adv.* 压倒性地，不可抵抗地
2 hither and thither   到处（向各方）。例如：She ran hither and thither in the orchard.（她在果园里到处跑。）
3 anguish /'æŋgwɪʃ/   *n.* 苦闷，痛苦
4 verge /vɜːdʒ/   *n.* 边缘
5 ecstasy /'ekstəsi/   *n.* 狂喜
6 unfathomable /ʌn'fæðəməbl/   *adj.* 深不可测的
7 prefiguring /ˌpriː'fɪɡərɪŋ/   *adj.* 预想的，预示的

三种激情

有三种激情，简单然而却异常强烈，它们控制着我的人生，那便是：对爱的渴望，对知识的追求，以及对人类苦难难以承受的同情。这三种激情像变化莫测的狂风肆意地把我刮来刮去，刮入痛苦的深海，到了绝望的边缘。

我寻求爱，首先是因为它能让我欣喜若狂 —— 这种喜悦之情如此强烈，使我常常宁愿为这几个小时的愉悦而牺牲生命中其他的一切。我寻求爱，还是因为爱能解除孤独 —— 在这种可怕的孤独中，一颗颤抖的良心在世界的边缘注视着冰冷、无底、死寂的深渊。我寻求爱，还因为在爱的融合中，我能以某种神秘的图像看到曾被圣人和诗人想象过的天堂里未来的景象。这就是我所追寻的东西，虽然这似乎对于人类的生命来说过于完美，但这确实是我最终发现的东西。

我怀着同样的激情去探寻知识，我渴望理解人心，渴望知道为何星星会闪烁，我还企

edge. I have wished to understand the hearts of men. I have wished to know why the stars shine. And I have tried to apprehend the Pythagorean power by which number holds sway above the flux. A little of this, but not much, I have achieved.

Love and knowledge, so far as they were possible, led upward toward the heavens. But always pity brought me back to earth. Echoes of cries of pain reverberate in my heart. Children in famine, victims tortured by oppressors, helpless old people a hated burden to their sons, and the whole world of loneliness, poverty, and pain make a mockery[1] of what human life should be. I long to alleviate the evil, but I cannot, and I too suffer.

This has been my life. I have found it worth living, and would gladly live it again if the chance were offered me.

1 mockery /ˈmɒkəri/ n. 嘲弄，笑柄，蔑视

图弄懂毕达哥拉斯所谓的用数字控制变化的力量，但在这方面，我只知道一点点。

爱和知识的力量引我接近天堂，但同情之心往往又把我拉回大地。痛苦的哭泣在我心中回响震荡。饥饿的儿童，被压迫、受折磨的人们，无助的、成为儿孙们讨厌的包袱的老人们，整个充满了孤独、贫穷和苦难的世界，所有这一切都是对人类理想生活的讽刺。我渴望消除一切邪恶，但我办不到，因为我自己也处于苦难之中。

这就是我的生活。我认为值得一过。而且，如果有第二次机会，我将乐意再过一次。

含英咀华

本文选自罗素的自传，文章开篇直入主题，说明人生的三种激情即对爱的渴望，对知识的追求，以及对人类苦难的同情。人生中虽然有不如意，虽然有各种困苦，作者仍积极乐观地鼓励大家去面对，人生需要激情，即使经历苦难，也"值得一过"。最后他在文章的结尾表明如果有机会重来，他还想再活一次。

John Fitzgerald Kennedy

约翰·菲茨杰拉德·肯尼迪

约翰·菲茨杰拉德·肯尼迪（1917~1963），美国第35任总统。他是美国颇具影响力的肯尼迪政治家族的一员，被视为美国自由主义的代表。肯尼迪在1946年~1960年期间曾先后任众议员和参议员，并于1960年当选为美国总统，成为美国历史上唯一信奉罗马天主教的总统。在他总统任期内的主要事件包括：猪湾入侵、古巴导弹危机、柏林墙的建立、太空竞赛、越南战争的早期活动以及美国民权运动。

Inaugural[1] Address (Excerpts)

就职演说（节选）

Vice President Johnson, Mr. Speaker, Mr. Chief Justice, President Eisenhower, Vice President Nixon, President Truman, reverend[2] clergy, fellow citizens:

　　We observe today not a victory of party, but a celebration of freedom — symbolizing an end, as well as a beginning — signifying renewal[3], as well as change. For I have sworn before you and Almighty God the same solemn oath[4] our forebears[5] prescribed nearly a century and three quarters ago.

　　The world is very different now. For man holds in his mortal hands the power to abolish[6] all forms of human poverty and all forms of human life. And yet the same revolutionary beliefs for which our forebears fought are still at issue[7] around the globe — the belief that the rights of man come not from the generosity of the state, but from the hand of God.

　　We dare not forget today that we are the

副总统约翰逊、议长先生、司法院长、艾森豪威尔总统、副总统尼克松、杜鲁门总统、尊敬的牧师神职人员、人民同胞们：

　　我们今天目睹的不是一个党派的胜利，而是一个自由的庆典——它象征着结束，也象征着开始——既意味着延续，也意味着变化。因为我已在你们和万能的上帝面前，依着我们先辈175年前写下的誓言宣誓。

　　世界已然今非昔比，因为人类手中已经掌握了力量，既可以用来消除各种形式的贫困，也可用以毁灭人类社会。然而，我们先辈曾为之战斗的那些革命性的信念在世界上依然受人争议——那就是，人权决非国家政权的慷慨施舍，而是上帝的赐予。

　　今天，我们不敢忘记，我们乃是那第一次革命的后裔。此时，让这个声音从这里同时传达给我们的朋友和敌人：火炬现已传递到新一代美国人手中——他们生于本世纪，既

1　inaugural /ɪˈnɔːgjərəl/　*adj.*　就职的
2　reverend /ˈrevərənd/　*adj.*　尊敬的
3　renewal /rɪˈnjuːəl/　*n.*　更新，革新，复兴
4　oath /əʊθ/　*n.*　誓言，誓约
5　forebear /ˈfɔːbeə(r)/　*n.*　祖先，祖宗
6　abolish /əˈbɒlɪʃ/　*v.*　废止，革除
7　at issue　在争论（中）。例如：The scientists are still at issue about the plan for building the space laboratory.（关于这项建造太空实验室的计划，科学家们的意见还不一致。）

heirs of that first revolution. Let the word go forth from this time and place, to friend and foe[1] alike, that the torch has been passed to a new generation of Americans — born in this century, tempered by war, disciplined by a hard and bitter peace, proud of our ancient heritage[2] — and unwilling to witness or permit the slow undoing of those human rights to which this Nation has always been committed, and to which we are committed today at home and around the world.

Let every nation know, whether it wishes us well or ill, that we shall pay any price, bear any burden, meet any hardship, support any friend, oppose any foe, in order to assure the survival and the success of liberty.

This much we pledge[3] — and more.

In your hands, my fellow citizens, more than in mine, will rest the final success or failure of our course. Since this country was founded, each generation of Americans has been summoned[4] to give testimony[5] to its national loyalty. The graves of young Americans who answered the call to service surround the globe.

Now the trumpet summons us again — not as a call to bear arms, though arms we need; not

经受过战火的锤炼，又经历过艰难严峻的和平岁月的考验。他们深为我们古老的遗产所自豪——决不愿目睹或听任诸项人权受到无形的侵蚀，这些权利被这个国家始终信守不渝，亦是我们正在国内和世界上捍卫的东西。

我要让每一个国家知道——无论他们对我们抱着善意还是敌意——我们都准备付出所有代价、承受所有责任、迎战所有艰险、支持所有朋友，对抗所有敌人，只为保证自由的存在和胜利。

这是我们矢志不渝的承诺，且远不止此！

我的同胞们，我们事业的最终成败将掌握在你们的手中而不仅仅是我的手中。从这个国家被创建那天起，每一代美国人都被召唤去证明自己对国家的忠诚。那些响应召唤献身国家的美国年轻人如今安息于世界的每个角落。

现在，召唤的号角再一次吹响——不是号召我们扛起武器，虽然武器是我们所需要的；也不是号召我们去参加战斗，虽然我们准备战斗——而是号召我们年复一年地去进行一场漫长而未分胜负的搏斗，

1 friend and foe 在这里，用了头韵（alliteration）的修辞方式。所谓头韵顾名思义，就是在一群字或诗中，第一个字母或发音的重复，如：pride and prejudice（傲慢与偏见）；sense and sensibility（情感与理智）等
2 heritage /ˈherɪtɪdʒ/ n. 遗产，继承物
3 pledge /pledʒ/ v. 保证，发誓
4 summon /ˈsʌmən/ v. 召唤，召集
5 testimony /ˈtestɪmənɪ/ n. 证言，证据

as a call to battle, though embattled we are — but a call to bear the burden of a long twilight struggle, year in and year out, "rejoicing in hope, patient in tribulation[1]" — a struggle against the common enemies of man: tyranny[2], poverty, disease, and war itself.

Can we forge[3] against these enemies a grand and global alliance, North and South, East and West, that can assure a more fruitful life for all mankind? Will you join in that historic effort?

In the long history of the world, only a few generations have been granted the role of defending freedom in its hour of maximum danger. I do not shank from this responsibility — I welcome it. I do not believe that any of us would exchange places with any other people or any other generation. The energy, the faith, the devotion which we bring to this endeavor will light our country and all who serve it — and the glow from that fire can truly light the world.

And so, my fellow Americans: ask not what your country can do for you — ask what you can do for your country.

My fellow citizens of the world: ask not what America will do for you, but what together we can do for the freedom of man.

Finally, whether you are citizens of America

1 tribulation /ˌtrɪbjuˈleɪʃn/ n. 苦难，灾难
2 tyranny /ˈtɪrəni/ n. 压制；统治；暴政
3 forge /fɔːdʒ/ v. 打制；想出；伪造

"在希望中欢乐，在患难中忍耐"——以反对人类共同的敌人：暴政、贫困、疾病以及战争本身。

为了反对这些敌人，我们能够将南方与北方、东方与西方团结起来，熔铸成一个伟大的全球性联盟，以确保全人类享有更为硕果累累的生活吗？你们愿意参与这项历史性的努力吗？

在漫长的世界史上，只有少数几代人在自由临危之际，被赋予保卫自由的使命。我不会逃避这种责任——我乐于接受。我也不相信我们中的任何人会愿意与其他国家的人民或其他时代的人民易地而处。我们为此所付出的精力、信念和奉献将照亮我们的国家和所有为国效力的人——而这把火的光辉也能够真正照亮全世界。

因此，我的美国同胞们：不要问你的国家可以为你做些什么，而应问你自己能为你的国家做些什么。

我的世界同胞们：不要问美国能为你们做些什么，而应问我们能够共同为全人类的自由做些什么。

最后，不论诸位是美国公民还是世界其他国家的公民，请

言近旨远　醍醐灌顶

or citizens of the world, ask of us the same high standards of strength and sacrifice which we ask of you. With a good conscience our only sure reward, with history the final judge of our deeds, let us go forth to lead the land we love, asking His blessing and His help, but knowing that here on earth God's work must truly be our own.

用我们对你们提出的高标准要求我们贡献力量，做出牺牲。良知是我们唯一可靠的报酬，历史终将裁决我们的功业，让我们迈步向前领导我们所挚爱的国家，在祈求神的赐福和神的帮助的同时深切体会，上帝在人间的工作要由我们亲手完成。

含英咀华

　　本文节选自肯尼迪在1961年1月20日的就职演说，在演说中，他呼吁美国民众应承担起更多的义务，做出更大的牺牲。他在演说中提到的"不要问你的国家可以为你做些什么，而应问你自己能为你的国家做些什么"成为了美国总统历次就职演说中最脍炙人口的语句之一，他的演说也成为20世纪最令人难忘的美国总统就职演说，是激励型语言和呼吁公民义务的典范之作。

韶华易逝
只争朝夕

Dale Carnegie
戴尔·卡耐基

戴尔·卡耐基（1888~1955），美国著名的心理学家和人际关系学家。他所开创的"人际关系训练班"遍布世界各地。他虽出生卑微，饱受奚落嘲笑，但最终选择了不断的自我磨炼，运用心理学知识对人类共同的心理特点进行探索和分析，开创和发展了一种融合演讲术、做人处世、推销和管理等的训练方式，影响了不同国籍、不同时代的千百万人。他的主要著作有《语言的突破》(The Quick and Easy Way to Effective Speaking, 1931)、《人性的光辉》(How to Win Friends and Influence People, 1936)、《人性的优点》(How to Stop Worrying and Start Living, 1948)等。他的作品曾被译成二十八种文字，其中《人性的弱点全集》(Lifetime Plan for Success, 1936)一书，是继《圣经》之后世界出版史上第二畅销书！

Live in "Day-Tight Compartments"

完全独立的今天

In the spring of 1871, a young man picked up a book and read twenty-one words that had a profound[1] effect on his future. A medical student at the Montreal General Hospital, he was worried about passing the final reexamination, worried about what to do, where to go, how to build up a practice, how to make a living.

The twenty-one words that this young medical student read in 1871 helped him to become the most famous physician of his generation. He organized the world-famous Johns Hopkins School of Medicine. He became Regius Professor[2] of Medicine at Oxford — the highest honor that can be bestowed[3] upon many medical men in the British Empire. He was knighted[4] by the King of England. When he died, two huge volumes containing 1,466 pages were required to tell the story of his life.

His name was Sir William Osier. Here are the twenty-one words that he read in the spring of 1871 — twenty-one words from Thomas Carlyle[5]

1871年春天，一个年轻人拿起了一本书，看到对他前途有莫大影响的21个字。他是蒙特利尔综合医院的医科学生，生活中充满了忧虑，担心怎样通过期末考试，担心该做些什么事情，该到哪去，怎样才能开业，怎样才能过活。

这位年轻的医科学生在1871年所读到的那句话使他成为那一代最有名的医学家。此后他创建了全世界知名的约翰霍普金斯医学院。他成为了牛津大学医学院的钦定讲座教授——这是在大英帝国学医的人所能得到的最高荣誉。他还被英王册封为爵士。在他死后，人们用了整整两大卷书——厚达1466页的篇幅，来记述他的一生。

他就是威廉·奥斯勒爵士。他在1871年春天所看到的那一句由托马斯·卡莱尔所写的话是："最重要的不是去看远方模糊的事，而是要去做手

---

1 profound /prəˈfaʊnd/ adj. 极深的，深奥的
2 Regius Professor 钦定讲座教授（尤指在牛津大学或剑桥大学，该职位由君主钦定设立或由君主批准任命）
3 bestow /bɪˈstəʊ/ v. 授予，适用
4 knight /naɪt/ v. 授以爵位
5 Thomas Carlyle 托马斯·卡莱尔（1795~1881），苏格兰评论、讽刺作家、历史学家。其作品在维多利亚时代甚具影响力，主要有《法国革命》（The French Revolution, 1858）、《过去与现在》（Past and Present, 1843）等

that helped him lead a life free from worry: "Our main business is not to see what lies dimly at a distance, but to do what lies clearly at hand."

Forty-two years later, on a soft spring night when the tulips were blooming on the campus, this man, Sir William Osier, addressed the students of Yale University. He told Yale students that a man like himself who had been a professor in four universities and had written a popular book was supposed to have "brains of a special quality". He declared that that was untrue. He said that his intimate friends knew that his brains were "of the most mediocre[1] character".

What, then, was the secret of his success? He stated that it was owing to what he called living in "day-tight compartments." What did he mean by that? A few months before he spoke at Yale, Sire William Osier had crossed the Atlantic on a great ocean liner where the captain standing on the bridge, could press a button and — presto[2]! — there was a clanging of machinery and various parts of ship were immediately shut off from one another — shut off into watertight compartments[3]. "Now each one of you," Dr. Osier said to those Yale students, "is a much more marvelous[4] organization than the great liner, and bound on a longer voyage. What I urge is that

---

1 mediocre /ˌmiːdɪˈəʊkə(r)/ *adj.* 平庸的，平凡的
2 presto *int.* 嘿！（表示完成某事如变戏法般容易、迅速）
3 compartment /kəmˈpɑːtmənt/ *n.* 间隔，隔间
4 marvelous /ˈmɑːvələs/ *adj.* 极好的，非凡的

边清楚的事。"

42年后，在一个温煦的春夜，那是郁金香开满校园的时候，威廉·奥斯勒爵士对耶鲁大学的学生发表了演讲。他对那些耶鲁大学的学生们说，像他这样一个曾经在四所大学当过教授，写过一本很受欢迎的书的人，似乎应该有"特殊的头脑"，但其实不然。他说他的一些好朋友都知道，他的脑筋其实是"最普通不过了"。

那么他成功的秘诀是什么呢？他认为这完全是因为自己活在一个所谓的"完全独立的今天"里。这是什么意思呢？在奥斯勒爵士到耶鲁去演讲的几个月之前，他乘着一艘很大的海轮横渡大西洋，他看见船长站在驾驶台前，按下一个按钮，听见一阵机械运转的声音，船的几个部分就立刻相互隔开，成为水密舱区。奥斯勒爵士对那些耶鲁大学的学生说："你们每个人的组织都要比那艘大海轮精美得多，所要走的航程也要远很多，我要劝各位的是，你们也要学着怎样控制一切，从而活在一个"完全独立的今天"里面，这是在航程中确保安全的最好方法。到驾驶台去，你会发现那

you so learn to control the machinery as to live with 'day-tight compartments' as the most certain way to ensure safety on the voyage. Get on the bridge, and see that at least the great bulkheads[1] are in working order. Touch a button and hear, at every level of your life, the iron doors shutting out the past — the dead yesterdays. Touch another and shut off, with a metal curtain, the future the unborn tomorrows. Then you are safe — safe for today! Shut off the past! Let the dead past bury its dead. Shut out the yesterdays which have lighted fools the way to dusty death. The load of tomorrow, added to that of yesterday, carried today, makes the strongest falter[2]. Shut off the future as tightly as the past. The future is today. There is no tomorrow. The day of man's salvation is now. Waste of energy, mental distress, nervous worries dog the steps of a man who is anxious about the future. Shut close, then the great fore and aft bulkheads, and prepare to cultivate[3] the habit of life of 'day-tight compartments'."

Did Dr. Osier mean to say that we should not make any effort to prepare for tomorrow? No, not at all. But he did go on in that address to say that the best possible way to prepare for tomorrow is to concentrate with all your intelligence, all your enthusiasm, on doing today's work superbly today. That is the only possible way

些大的隔舱至少都可以独立使用；按下按钮，注意你生活的每一个层面，用铁门把过去隔断——隔断已经死去的那些昨天；按下另一个按钮，用铁门把未来也隔断——隔断那些尚未诞生的明天。然后你就保险了——你有的是今天！切断过去，将已死的过去埋葬掉。切掉那些会把傻子引上死亡之路的昨天。昨天与明天的担忧会成为今天最大的障碍。要把未来像过去一样紧紧地关在门外。未来就在于今天，根本就没有叫做明天的东西，人类得到救赎的日子就是现在。精力的浪费、精神的苦闷，情绪的紧张，都会紧随一个为未来担忧的人，那么，把船里的大隔舱都关断吧，准备养成一个好习惯，生活在'完全独立的今天'里。"

奥斯勒爵士是不是想说我们不应该为明天下工夫准备呢？不是的，绝不是这样。在那次演讲里，他还说了：为明日准备的最好方法，就是要集中你所有的智慧，所有的热忱，把今天的工作做得尽善尽美，这就

---

1 bulkhead /'bʌlkhed/   n.   隔壁；防水壁
2 falter /'fɔːltə, 'fɒl-/   v.   衰弱；畏缩
3 cultivate /'kʌltɪveɪt/   v.   培养；耕作

you can prepare for the future.

By all means take thought for the tomorrow, yes, careful thought and planning and preparation. But have no anxiety.

So, the first thing you should know about worry is this: if you want to keep it out of your life, do what Sire William Osier did — "Shut the iron doors on the past and the future. Live in Day-tight Compartments."

是你能应付未来的唯一方法。

一定要为明天着想，不错，人们应该考虑周到，做好一切计划和准备。可是，千万不要忧虑。

因此，面对忧虑，你首先明白的就是：如果你想让它远离你的生活，就要学习威廉·奥斯勒爵士所说的那句话——"用铁门把过去和未来阻断，生活在完全独立的今天"。

含英咀华

在本文中，卡耐基用船来比喻人生，告诉读者与其期待明天不如抓住今天，从眼前做起，必将到达成功的彼岸。但最后作者又强调，重视今天不等于抛弃明天：只是要拥有更好的明天，就要将今天该做的一切做好，为明天打下一个良好的基础。文章比喻新颖独特，简单易懂，读后引人深思。

William Lyon Phelps
威廉·里昂·费尔浦斯

威廉·里昂·费尔浦斯（1865~1943），美国耶鲁大学教授与学者，以博学与智慧闻名于世，著作涉及小说理论研究等方面，著有《现代小说家评论集》(Essays on Modern Novelists, 1910)等。

To Be or Not to Be

"To be or not to be" Outside the Bible, these six words are the most famous in all the literature of the world. They were spoken by Hamlet when he was thinking alone, and they are the most famous words in Shakespeare because Hamlet was speaking not only for himself but also for every thinking man and woman. To be or not be — to live or not to live; to live richly and abundantly and eagerly, or to live dully and meanly and scarcely. A philosopher once wanted to know whether he was alive or not, which is a good question for everyone to put himself occasionally. He answered it by saying, "I think, therefore I am."

But the best definition of existence I ever saw was one given by another philosopher who said: "To be is to be in relations." If this is true, then the more relations a living thing has, the more it is alive. To live abundantly means simply to increase the range and intensity of our relations. Unfortunately we are so constituted that we get to love our routine. But apart from our regular occupation how much are we alive? If you are interested only in your regular occupation, you are alive only to that extent. So far as other things are concerned — poetry and prose, music, pictures, sports,

生存还是毁灭

"生存还是毁灭"除《圣经》外，这六个字便是整个世界文学中最有名的六个字了。这六个字是哈姆雷特一次喃喃自语时说的，而这六个字也成了莎士比亚作品中最有名的几个字，因为哈姆雷特不仅道出了他自己的心声，同时也代表了一切有思想的人的心声。是活还是不活——是生存还是死亡，是要生活得丰满充实、兴致勃勃，还是活得枯燥委琐、贫乏无味。一位哲人曾想弄清自己是否活着，这个问题也值得每个人不时思考。这位哲学家对此的答案是："我思，故我在。"

但是我所见过的关于存在的最好的定义却来自另一位哲学家，他说："生活即是联系。"如果这话不假的话，那么一个有生命者的联系越多，它也就越有活力。所谓要活得丰富充实也即是要扩大和加强我们的各种联系。不幸的是，我们却安于陈规俗套。试问除去我们的日常工作，我们的真

unselfish friendships, politics, international affairs — you are dead.

Contrariwise[1], it is true that every time you acquire a new interest — even more, a new accomplishment — you increase your power of life. No one who is deeply interested in a large variety of subjects can remain unhappy; the real pessimist[2] is the person who had lost interest.

Bacon said that a man dies as often as he loses a friend, but we gain new life by contacts, new friends. What is supremely true of living objects is no less true of ideas, which are also alive. Where your thoughts are, there will your life be also. If your thoughts are confined only to your business, only to your physical welfare, only to the narrow circle of the town in which you live, then you live in a narrow circumscribed life. But if you are interested in what is going on in China, then you are living in China; if you're interested in the characters of a good novel, then you are living with those highly interesting people; if you listen intently to fine music, you are away from your immediate surroundings and living in a world of passion and imagination.

---

1 contrariwise /ˈkɒntreərɪwaɪz/　*adv.*　反之
2 pessimist /ˈpesɪmɪst/　*n.*　悲观主义

正生活又有多少?如果你只是对你的日常工作才有兴趣，那你的生命也就很有限了。至于在其他事物方面，比如诗歌、散文、音乐、美术、体育、无私的友谊、政治与国际事务——你却漠不关心。

但反过来说，每当你获得一种新的兴趣——甚至一项新的造诣——你就增长了你的生活本领。一个能对许许多多事物都深感兴趣的人是不可能总不愉快的，真正的悲观者只能是那些丧失兴趣的人。

培根曾讲过，一个人失去朋友即是死亡。但是凭着交往，凭着新友，我们就能获得再生。这条对于生命可谓千真万确的道理在一定程度上也完全适用于人的思想，思想也是有生命的。你的思想所在便是你的生命所在。如果你的思想只局限于你的业务范围，局限于你的物质利益，局限于你所在城镇的狭隘圈子，那么你的一生便也只是受着多方局限的狭隘的一生。但是如果你对当前中国哪里所发生的种种感兴趣，那么你便可说也活在中国；如果你对一本绝妙小说中的人物感兴趣，你便是活在一批极有趣的人们中间；如果你能全神贯注地倾听美好的音乐，你就会超脱出你的周围环境而活在一个充满激情与想象的世界之中。

To be or not to be — to live intensely and richly, or merely to exist, that depends on ourselves. Let's widen and intensify our relations. While we live, let us live!

生存还是毁灭——是活得热烈活得丰富，还是只是简单存在，这全在我们自己。但愿我们都能不断扩展和增强我们的各种联系。只要我们活一天，就要精彩一天！

含英咀华

　　本文语言简洁精练，自然纯朴。作者首先引用莎士比亚的"to be or not to be"开篇，引出本文的中心论点：是要生活还是不要生活，是要生活得丰满充实、兴致勃勃，还是只是活得枯燥委琐、贫乏无味。然后引经据典，引用读者耳熟能详的名言来讲述人生哲理。文章处处闪烁着作者的智慧，充分展示了作者的博学与机智，语言简洁精练、自然纯朴，结尾处又重申文章的主题：但愿我们都能不断扩展和增强我们的各种联系。全文行文流畅，可谓水到渠成。

Orison Marden
奥里森·马登

奥里森·马登（1848~1924）是美国《成功》(*Success Magazine*)杂志的创办人，被公认为美国成功学的奠基人和最伟大的成功励志大师。他所提供的成功学原理，曾在美国引起强烈的反响，并改变了许多人的命运，也成就了许多成功人物，他是一个用自己的奋斗经验激励年轻人成功的大师。他的书鞭辟入里，剖析透彻，读起来令人精神振奋。

The Sunshine-Man (Excerpts)

"There's the dearest little old gentleman," says James Buckham, "who goes into town every morning on the 8:30 train. I don't know his name, and yet I know him better than anybody else in town. He just radiates[1] cheerfulness as far as you can see him. There is always a smile on his face, and I never heard him open his mouth except to say something kind, courteous, or good natured. Everybody bows to him, even strangers, and he bows to everybody, yet never with the slightest hint of presumption[2] or familiarity. If the weather is fine, his jolly compliments make it seem finer; and if it is raining, the merry way in which he speaks of it is as good as a rainbow." Everybody who goes in on the 8:30 train knows the sunshine-man; it's his train. You just hurry up a little, and I'll show you the sunshine-man this morning. It's foggy and cold, but if one look at him doesn't cheer you up so that you'll want to whistle, then I'm no judge of human nature."

---

1 radiate /'reɪdieɪt/ v. 显出，流露
2 presumption /prɪ'zʌmpʃn/ n. 放肆；推测

让心中充满阳光
（节选）

美国作家詹姆斯·巴克海姆曾这样回忆一个人："有一位个子矮小的老人十分有趣，每天早晨，他都会乘八点三十分的火车去镇上。我不知道他叫什么，可我是镇上最了解他的人。只要老人进入你的视线，他就会向你传达快乐。老人总是一副笑意融融的样子，我几乎没有听过他说话，可每次开口，他的语气都是十分和蔼、谦逊、慈祥的。路过的人都会向老人点头打招呼，甚至陌生人也是一样；老人也向所有人点头回敬，但从未显现出丝毫的傲慢或放肆之意。在阳光灿烂的日子，他那令人欢快的问候声会使阳光愈加明媚；换作是雨天的话，他提到天气时的乐观语气则如同彩虹一样美丽。"每个乘坐八点三十分火车的人都知道这位阳光老人，这是他的火车。你要快一点，我会给你指出这位阳光老人。虽是大雾和严寒的天气，但如果你看见他都不会振作起来想吹口哨的话，那么我就无法鉴别人性了。

45

"Good morning, sir!" said Mr. Jolliboy in going to the same train.

"Why, sir, I don't know you," replied Mr. Neversmile.

"I didn't say you did, sir. Good morning, sir!" "The inborn geniality¹ of some people," says Whipple amounts to² genius. "How in our troubled lives," asks J. Freeman Clarke, "could we do without these fair, sunny natures, into which on their creation-day God allowed nothing sour, acrid, or bitter to enter, but made them a perpetual solace³ and comfort by their cheerfulness?" There are those whose very presence carries sunshine with them wherever they go; a sunshine which means pity for the poor, sympathy for the suffering, help for the unfortunate, and benignity⁴ toward all.

Everybody loves the sunny soul. His very face is a passport anywhere. All doors fly open to him. He disarms prejudice and envy, for he bears good will to everybody. He is as welcome in every household as the sunshine.

"He was quiet, cheerful, genial⁵" says Carlyle in his "Reminiscences" concerning Edward Irving's sunny helpfulness. "His soul unruffled⁶, clear as a mirror, honestly loving and

---

1 geniality /ˌdʒiːniˈæləti/ n. 温和，舒适，亲切
2 amount to 总计，等于。His words amount to a refusal. 他说的话等于是拒绝。
3 solace /ˈsɒləs/ n. 安慰
4 benignity /bɪˈnɪɡnəti/ n. 仁慈，善行
5 genial /ˈdʒiːniəl/ adj. 和蔼的，亲切的
6 unruffled /ʌnˈrʌfld/ adj. 镇定的，平静的

"早上好，先生！"前往同一列车的吉利伯尔先生说。

"什么，先生，我不认识你。""永不言笑"先生回答。

"我没有说你认识我，先生。先生，早上好！"

惠普尔说："有些人与生俱来的亲切感本身就是一种天赋。"弗里曼·克拉克问道："在我们的生活陷入困境的情况下，如果没有这些公正、阳光的本性，我们该怎么办呢？在上帝造人的时候不让敌意、尖刻或痛苦侵犯这种本性，而是让人们的欢乐使他们永远得到安慰和鼓舞。"有一些人，不管身在何处，阳光都会跟着他们的步履；这里的阳光意味着对穷人的怜悯、对痛苦者的同情、对不幸者的帮助以及对所有人的仁慈。

每个人都喜欢阳光乐观的人。他的笑脸就是万能的护照，所有的大门都为他开启；他能消除骄傲和嫉妒，因为他赋予每个人好心情；所有家庭都像喜欢阳光一样喜欢他。

在自己的回忆录里，英国作家卡莱尔写到了艾德华·欧文乐观向上的性格："他十分沉静、乐观、亲切。他的心灵仿佛镜子一般平滑、清亮，他真心地爱别人，也被别人所

loved, Irving's voice was to me one of blessedness and new hope."

And to William Wilberforce the poet Southey paid this tribute: "I never saw any other man who seemed to enjoy such perpetual serenity[1] and sunshine of spirit."

"I resolved," said Tom Hood, "that, like the sun, so long as my day lasted, I would look on the bright side of everything."

When Goldsmith was in Flanders he discovered the happiest man he had ever seen. At his toil, from morning till night, he was full of song and laughter. Yet this sunny-hearted being was a slave, maimed[2], deformed, and wearing a chain. How well he illustrated that saying which bids us, if there is no bright side, to polish up the dark one! "Mirth is like the flash of lightning that breaks through the gloom of the clouds and glitters for a moment; cheerfulness keeps up a daylight in the soul, filling it with a steady and perpetual serenity." It is cheerfulness that has the staying quality, like the sunshine changing a world of gloom into a paradise of beauty.

The first prize at a flower-show was taken by a pale, sickly little girl, who lived in a close, dark court in the east of London. The judges asked how she could grow it in such a dingy and sunless place. She replied that a little ray of sunlight came into the court; as soon as it appeared in

1 serenity /sə'renəti/ *n.* 宁静，沉着
2 maim /meɪm/ *v.* 使残废，使不能工作

爱；对我来说欧文的声音就是一种祝福和新的希望。"

对于威廉·威尔伯福斯，英国著名诗人骚赛曾这样表达自己的敬佩之情："除了他，我从未见过其他人享受精神上的永恒的平静和快乐。"

"我决定了，"汤姆·胡德说，"就像太阳一样，只要我活着，我就会看到每件事情光明的一面。"

在弗兰德斯期间，英国作家戈德史密斯遇到了一个他所见过的最快乐的人。虽然日夜不停地埋头干活，他却总是欢歌笑语不停。这个阳光向上的人却是一个奴隶，而且身体残废、面目丑陋，还带着镣铐。他很好地解释了那句我们深省的话——假如看不到光明的一面，就去驱除阴暗的一面吧。"欢笑，就像是一道闪电，透过云层的阴暗，短暂地闪烁着；快乐在你的心中播撒阳光，使其永远平静安详。"只有快乐永远具有这样的品质，犹如阳光可以将黯淡的世界变成美丽的天堂。

在一次花展上，一个苍白的、瘦弱的小女孩获得了第一名。她的家在伦敦东区一个拥挤、阴暗的庭院里。评委问

the morning, she put her flower beneath it, and, as it moved, moved the flower, so that she kept it in the sunlight all day.

"Water, air, and sunshine, the three greatest hygienic[1] agents, are free, and within the reach of all." "Twelve years ago," says Walt Whitman, "I came to Camden to die. But every day I went into the country, and bathed in the sunshine, lived with the birds and squirrels, and played in the water with the fishes. I received my health from Nature."

"It is the unqualified result of all my experience with the sick," said Florence Nightingale, "that second only to their need of fresh air, is their need of light; that, after a close room, what most hurts them is a dark room; and that it is not only light, but direct sunshine they want."

"Sunlight," says Dr. L. W. Curtis, in "Health Culture," "has much to do in keeping air in a healthy condition. No plant can grow in the dark; neither can man remain healthy in a dark, ill-ventilated room. When the first asylum for the blind was erected in Massachusetts, the committee decided to save expense by not having any windows. They reasoned that, as the patients could not see, there was no need of any light. It was built without windows, but ventilation was well provided for, and the poor sightless

---

1 hygienic /haɪˈdʒiːnɪk/ *adj.* 卫生学的，卫生的

她如何能在这样一个阴暗、缺少光照的地方培育出花朵，小女孩的回答是：庭院内只有一缕阳光，每天早上只要太阳出来，她就让花接触这缕阳光，然后随着光线的改变，不断地挪动花盆，这样，她的花就一整天都在阳光的照射下了。

"水，空气和阳光，是最有益于健康的三种物质，而且可以任意索取，触手可及。"沃尔特·惠特曼说，"十二年前，我打算去坎登等待死亡。但因为我每天在乡村里散步，在阳光里沐浴，与小鸟和松鼠为伴，在水中和鱼儿嬉戏，最后我居然从大自然中重新获得了健康。"

"从我照顾病人的所有经验来看，"弗罗伦斯·南丁格尔说，"有人说除了对新鲜空气的需要，病人最需要的是灯光，这种观点是不对的。除了密封的房间，黑暗的房间对病人伤害最大；他们需要的不只是灯光，更需要的是直接接触阳光。"

柯蒂斯博士在其"健康文化"一文中说道，"阳光与保持健康的空气有很大关系。没有植物可以在黑暗中生长；人类也不能在黑暗通风不好的房间里保持健康。当第一个盲人收容所

patients were domiciled in the house. But things did not go well: one after another began to sicken, and great languor[1] fell upon them; they felt distressed and restless, craving something, they hardly knew what. After two had died and all were ill, the committee decided to have windows. The sunlight poured in, and the white faces recovered their color; their flagging energies and depressed spirits revived, and health was restored."

The sun, making all living things to grow, exerts its happiest influence[2] in cheering the mind of man and making his heart glad, and if a man has sunshine in his soul he will go on his way rejoicing; content to look forward if under a cloud, not bating one jot of heart or hope if for a moment cast down; honoring his occupation, whatever it be; rendering even rags respectable by the way he wears them; and not only happy himself, but giving happiness to others.

How a man's face shines when illuminated by a great moral motive! And his manner, too, is touched with the grace of light.

在马萨诸塞州建立时，委员会为节省开支，决定不安窗户。他们的理由是，因为病人看不见，所以不需要光亮。收容所虽然没有窗户，但通风条件良好，可怜的盲人们就居住在这样的房子里。但是糟糕的事发生了：盲人一个接一个地开始生病，变得非常衰弱无力；他们感到痛苦和不安，渴望某种东西，但他们却不知道那是什么。在两个人相继去世和所有人都生病后，委员会决定安装窗户。阳光涌入房中，苍白的脸恢复了以往的红润；他们衰弱的精力和沮丧的精神重新焕发起来，身体也康复了。

太阳促使万物生长，同时也给人施以最快乐的影响，人们才得以精神焕发、心情愉快。假如一个人心中拥有阳光，他就会踏上幸福之路；在压力重重时也乐意向前看，就算有片刻沮丧，也不会丧失丝毫的精神力量或希望；珍惜自己所拥有的一切；就算衣衫褴褛，也感激不尽；不但自己快乐，也把快乐传递给他人。

当被一个伟大的道德动机照亮时，一个人是多么光彩照人！他的举止也充满着优雅的光芒。

---

1 languor /ˈlæŋɡə(r)/ *n.* 倦怠，疲倦，无气力
2 exert...influence 影响……

含英咀华

在本文中，作者运用了大量的实例和事实来告诉读者人生虽然苦乐参半，但只要我们端正态度，只要我们心中充满阳光，快乐就会围绕在我们身边，并且我们也会将快乐传递下去。而快乐是与金钱，财富，自由，厄运都无关的东西，快乐就在于你自己，如果你的心中如本文所提到的那些人一样充满阳光，你的人生就是快乐的，你会用快乐换来你想得到的东西。

海伦·凯勒

海伦·凯勒（1880~1968），美国聋哑女作家和教育家。她是一个生活在黑暗中却又给人类带来光明的女性，一个度过了生命的88个春秋，却熬过了87年无光、无声、无语的孤独岁月的弱女子。然而，正是这么一个幽闭在盲聋哑世界里的人，竟然毕业于哈佛大学德吉利夫学院，并用生命的全部力量处处奔走，建起了一家家慈善机构，为残疾人造福，被美国《时代周刊》(Time)评选为20世纪美国十大英雄偶像。她能创造这一奇迹，全靠一颗不屈不挠的心。海伦接受了生命的挑战，用爱心去拥抱世界，以惊人的毅力面对困境，终于在黑暗中找到了光明，最后又把慈爱的双手伸向全世界。

Three Days to See (Excerpts)

假如给我三天光明
（节选）

All of us have read thrilling stories in which the hero had only a limited and specified time to live. Sometimes it was as long as a year, sometimes as short as 24 hours. But always we were interested in discovering just how the doomed man chose to spend his last days or his last hours. I speak, of course, of free men who have a choice, not condemned[1] criminals whose sphere[2] of activities is strictly delimited[3].

Such stories set us thinking, wondering what we should do under similar circumstances. What events, what experiences, what associations should we crowd into those last hours as mortal beings? What happiness should we find in reviewing the past, what regrets?

Sometimes I have thought it would be an excellent rule to live each day as if we should die tomorrow. Such an attitude would emphasize sharply the values of life. We should live each day with a gentleness, a vigor and a keenness of appreciation which are often lost when time stretches before us in the constant panorama[4] of more days and months and years to come.

我们大家都读过一些令人兴奋激动的故事，这些故事里的主人公只能再活一段有限的时光，有时长达一年，有时却只有短短的24个小时。但是在探究这个即将离开人世者选择怎样度过他最后岁月的问题上，我们总是饶有兴趣。当然，我说的是有选择权利的自由人而不是死刑犯。死刑犯的活动范围是严格受限制的。

这样的故事让我们思考，想想在相似的情况下，我们该怎么办？临死之时，什么样的事情、体验、关系应该被放入最后的时光中呢？回忆往昔，什么使我们开心快乐？什么又使我们抱憾呢？

有时，我常这样想，把每天都当临终的前一天去生活，这或许是一个好的习惯。这种态度可以鲜明地强调生命的价值。我们应该生活得优雅

---

1 condemn /kən'dem/ v. 判刑，责备，处刑
2 sphere /sfɪə(r)/ n. 范围，领域；球，球体
3 delimit /di'lɪmɪt/ v. 定界限，划界
4 panorama /ˌpænə'rɑːmə/ n. 全景

There are those, of course, who would adopt the Epicurean[1] motto of "Eat, drink, and be merry". But most people would be chastened by the certainty of impending[2] death.

In stories the doomed hero is usually saved at the last minute by some stroke of fortune, but almost always his sense of values is changed. He becomes more appreciative of the meaning of life and its permanent spiritual values. It has often been noted that those who live, or have lived, in the shadow of death bring a mellow[3] sweetness to everything they do.

Most of us, however, take life for granted. We know that one day we must die, but usually we picture that day as far in the future. When we are in buoyant[4] health, death is all but unimaginable. We seldom think of it. The days stretch out in an endless vista[5]. So we go about our petty tasks, hardly aware of our listless attitude toward life.

The same lethargy[6], I am afraid, characterizes the use of all our faculties and senses. Only the

---

1 Epicurean /ˌepɪkjʊ(ə)ˈriːən/   *adj.*   好享乐的，享乐主义的（注：伊壁鸠鲁是古希腊哲学家，他认为生活的主题目的是享乐，而最高的享受唯通过合理的生活，如自我控制才能得到。因为生活享受的目的被过分强调，而达此目的之手段被忽视，所以伊壁鸠鲁的信徒现今变为追求享乐的人。他们的信条是："让我们吃喝，因为明天我们就死亡。"）

2 impending /ɪmˈpendɪŋ/   *adj.*   逼迫的，迫切的，悬空的
3 mellow /ˈmeləʊ/   *adj.*   成熟的，醇香的，熟练的
4 buoyant /ˈbɔɪənt/   *adj.*   有浮力的，心情愉快的
5 vista /ˈvɪstə/   *n.*   景色，景观
6 lethargy /ˈleθədʒi/   *n.*   冷漠；无精打采

从容、精力充沛、观察敏锐，而这些将会日复一日，月复一月，年复一年慢慢失去。当然，也有人愿按伊壁鸠鲁的信条"吃、喝和欢乐"去生活。但绝大多数人还是被即将面临死亡的必然性所折磨。

在故事里，注定要死的主人公往往在最后一刻由某种命运的突变而得救，并且从此以后他的价值观被改变了。他变得更加理解生活的意义和它永恒的精神价值了。我们常常看到一些人，即使生活在死亡的阴影下，仍然对他所做的每件事情充满了甜美的感情。

但是，我们大多数人把生活认为是理所当然的。我们知道，某一天我们一定会死，但通常我们把那天想象在遥远的将来。当我们心宽体健时，死亡几乎是不可想象的，我们很少想到它。日子过得好像没有尽头，于是我们干着琐碎的事情，几乎意识不到我们对生活的倦怠态度。

我担心同样的冷漠也存在于我们对自己所有官能和意识的使用上。只有聋子才珍惜听力，唯有瞎子才体会到能看见事物的种种幸福，这种结论特别适合于那些在成年阶段失去

deaf appreciate hearing, only the blind realize the manifold[1] blessings that lie in sight. Particularly does this observation apply to those who have lost sight and hearing in adult life. But those who have never suffered impairment[2] of sight or hearing seldom make the fullest use of these blessed faculties. Their eyes and ears take in all sights and sounds hazily, without concentration and with little appreciation. It is the same old story of not being grateful for what we have until we lose it, of not being conscious of health until we are ill.

I have often thought it would be a blessing if each human being were stricken blind and deaf for a few days at some time during his early adult life. Darkness would make him more appreciative of sight; silence would teach him the joys of sound.

Now and then I have tested my seeing friends to discover what they see.

Recently I was visited by a very good friend who had just returned from a long walk in the woods, and I asked her what she had observed. "Nothing particular," she replied. I might have been incredulous[3] had I not been accustomed to such reposes, for long ago I became convinced that the seeing see little.

How was it possible, I asked myself, to walk for an hour through the woods and see nothing

视力和听力的人们，而那些从没有遭受视觉或听觉损伤之苦的人却很少充分利用这些天赐的官能。他们心不在焉，也不太感兴趣用眼睛和耳朵模糊地看着和听着周围的一切。正如人们不知道珍惜自己拥有的，直到失去时才明白它的价值一样，人们只有在生病时，才意识到健康的好处。

我常常想，如果每个人在他成年的早期生活中，有一段时间致盲致聋，那会是一种幸事，黑暗会使他更珍惜视力，寂静会教会他享受声音的美妙。

我不时地询问过我的能看见东西的朋友们，以了解他们看到什么。

最近，我的一个很好的朋友来看我，她刚从一片森林里散了很长时间的步回来，我问她看到了什么，她答道："没什么特别的。"如果我不是习惯了听到这种回答，我都可能不相信，因为很久以来我已确信这个情况：能看得见的人却看不到什么。

怎么可能呢，我问自己，在林子里逛了一个小时却没有发现任何值得欣赏的东西。我自己，一个不能看见东西的

1 manifold /'mænɪfəʊld/　adj.　多种的；有许多种类的
2 impairment /ɪm'peəmənt/　n.　损伤（毁损）
3 incredulous /ɪn'kredjələs/　adj.　怀疑的，不轻信的

worthy of noting? I who cannot see find hundreds of things to interest me through mere touch. I feel the delicate symmetry[1] of a leaf. I pass my hands lovingly about the smooth skin of a silver birch[2], or the rough, shaggy[3] bark of a pine. In the spring I touch the branches of trees hopefully in search of a bud the first sign of awakening Nature after her winter's sleep. I feel the delightful, velvety[4] texture[5] of a flower, and discover its remarkable convolutions[6]; and something of the miracle of Nature is revealed to me. Occasionally, if I am very fortunate, I place my hand gently on a small tree and feel the happy quiver[7] of a bird in full song. I am delighted to have the cool water of a brook[8] rush through my open finger. To me a lush carpet of pine needles or spongy[9] grass is more welcome than the most luxurious Persian[10] rug. To me the pageant of seasons is a thrilling and unending drama, the action of which streams through my finger tips.

At times my heart cries out with longing to see all these things. If I can get so much pleasure from mere touch, how much more beauty must be revealed by sight. Yet, those

人，仅仅通过触觉，都发现了许许多多令我感兴趣的东西。我感触到一片树叶完美的对称性。我充满爱意地抚摸过一株白桦那光滑的树皮，或一棵松树的粗糙树皮。春天，我摸着树干的枝条满怀希望地搜索着嫩芽，那是严冬的沉睡后，大自然苏醒的第一个迹象。我抚摸过花朵那令人愉快的天鹅绒般的质地，感觉到它那奇妙的卷绕，一些大自然的奇迹展示在我的眼前。有时，如果我很幸运，我把手轻轻地放在一棵小树上，还能感受到一只高声歌唱的小鸟的愉快颤抖。我十分快乐地让小溪涧的凉水穿过我张开的手指流淌过去。对我来说，一片茂密的地毯式的松针叶或松软而富弹性的草地比最豪华的波斯地毯更受欢迎。对我来说四季的壮观而华丽的展示是一部令人激动的、无穷尽的戏剧。这部戏剧的表演，通过我的手指尖流淌出来。

时而，我会因为渴望看到一切事物而在心中哭泣。如果说仅凭触觉我就能感受到这么多的愉快，那么凭视觉该有多少美丽的东西显露出来。然而，那些能看见的人明显看得很少，充满世间的色彩和动作的

---

1 symmetry /ˈsɪmɪtri/ n. 对称（性），匀称，整齐
2 birch /bɜːtʃ/ n. 桦树，桦木，桦条
3 shaggy /ˈʃægi/ adj. 毛发蓬松的，表面粗糙的
4 velvety /ˈvelvəti/ adj. 像天鹅绒的，轻软光滑的
5 texture /ˈtekstʃə(r)/ n. （材料等的）结构，质地
6 convolution /ˌkɒnvəˈluːʃn/ n. 回旋，卷曲，盘绕
7 quiver /ˈkwɪvə/ n. 震动，颤抖
8 brook /brʊk/ n. 小河，溪
9 spongy /ˈspʌndʒi/ adj. 海绵似的；不坚实的
10 Persian /ˈpɜːʃn/ adj. 波斯的（波斯人的）

who have eyes apparently see little. The panorama of color and action which fills the world is taken for granted. It is human, perhaps, to appreciate little that which we have and to long for that which we have not, but it is a great pity that in the world of light the gift of sight is used only as a mere conveniences rather than as a means of adding fullness to life.

景象被当成理所当然，或许，这可能是人性共有的特点；对我们具有的不怎么欣赏，而对我们不具有的却渴望得到。然而，这是一个极大的遗憾，在光明的世界里，视力的天赋仅仅作为一种方便之用，而没有作为增添生活美满的手段。

含英咀华

在本文中，海伦·凯勒用朴实的语言，发自内心地向我们揭示了一个哲理：拥有的东西我们可能不会珍惜，倘若失去我们就会认识到它的珍贵。假如我们每一个人都能像海伦·凯勒一样，在有生之年把对知识的渴求，看做对人生的追求，每天都抱着这种追求，怀着友善、朝气、渴望去生活，我们的人生将会增添多少欢乐、多少幸福啊！

态度
决定一切

Cecil Day Lewis
塞西尔·戴·刘易斯

塞西尔·戴·刘易斯（1904～1972）是英国最杰出的诗人之一，荣登1950年"女王荣誉名录"，获最优秀不列颠帝国勋章。他曾就读于舍伯恩中学和牛津的沃德姆学院。在大学时期，他结识了斯蒂芬·斯彭德和威斯坦·于格·奥登，后者对他早期的诗歌创作产生了深刻的影响。1951年刘易斯先生当选为牛津大学诗歌教授。他不仅在诗歌上很有建树，而且在写侦探小说方面也很有成就。其主要作品有《必死无疑》(Thou Shell of Death，1936)、《讨厌的雪人》(The Case of the Abominable Snowman, 1941)、《纠缠的网》(A Tangled Web, 1956)、《人生的结束》(End of Chapter, 1957)等。

I Wish I Could Believe

"The Best lack all conviction,

While the worse are full of passionate intensity."

THOSE TWO LINES of Yeats for me sum up the matter as it stands today when the very currency of belief seems debased[1]. I was brought up in the Christian church. Later I believed for a while that communism[2] offered the best hope for this world. I acknowledge the need for belief, but I cannot forget how through the ages great faiths have been vitiated by fanaticism[3] and dogmatism, by intolerance and cruelty, by the intellectual dishonesty, the folly, the crankiness or the opportunism of their adherents.

Have I no faith at all, then? Faith is the thing at the core of you, the sediment[4] that's left when hopes and illusions are drained away. The thing for which you make any sacrifice because without it you would be nothing — a mere walking shadow. I know what my own core is. I would in the last resort sacrifice any human relationship, any way of living to the search for truth which produces my poem. I know

我希望我能相信

"优秀的人们信心尽失，坏蛋们则充满了炙热的狂热。"

对我来说，叶芝的这两行诗概括了今天的现实，信仰的货币似乎已经贬值了。我是在基督教的熏陶下长大的，后来有一段时间我相信共产主义给这个世界带来了最大的希望。我承认信仰的必要性，但我无法忘记这些年来伟大的信仰是如何因其拥护者的狂热、教条、不容异说、残忍、学术欺诈、愚蠢、偏执或机会主义而遭到损害的。

那么，难道我就没有信仰吗？信仰存在于你的心灵深处，当希望和幻想渐渐枯竭，沉淀下来的就是信仰。为了它，你甘愿做出任何牺牲，因为没有它，你的存在就毫无意义——你只不过是一个会行走的影子。我知道我的内心深处有什么。在别无选择的情况

---

1 debased /dɪ'beɪst/　adj.　质量低劣的
2 communism /'kɒmjʊnɪz(ə)m/　n.　共产主义
3 fanaticism /fə'nætɪsɪz(ə)m/　n.　狂热，盲信
4 sediment /'sedɪm(ə)nt/　n.　沉淀物

there are heavy odds against any poem I write surviving after my death. I realize that writing poetry may seem the most preposterously useless thing a man can be doing today. Yet it is just at such times of crisis that each man discovers or rediscovers what he values most. My poet's instinct to make something comes out most strongly then, enabling me to use fear, doubt, even despair as creative stimuli. In doing so, I feel my kinship with humanity, with the common man who carries on doing his job till the bomb falls or the sea closes over him. Carries on because of his belief, however inarticulate[1], that this is the best thing he can do. But the poet is luckier than the layman, for his job is always a vocation. Indeed, it's so like a religious vocation that he may feel little need for a religious faith, but because it is always trying to get past the trivial and the transient[2] or to reveal these as images of the essential and the permanent, poetry is at least a kind of spiritual activity.

Men need a religious belief to make sense out of life. I wish I had such a belief myself, but any creed of mine would be honeycombed with confusions and reservations. Yet when I write a poem I am trying to make sense out of life. And just now and then my experience composes and transmutes[3] itself into a poem which tells

下，我愿意牺牲任何人际关系、任何生活方式去寻找使我能创作诗歌的真理。我知道很有可能我写的每一首诗在我死后都不能流传。我也明白诗歌创作在今天或许是一个人所能做得最荒谬、最无用的事情。然而，正是在这样的危难之时，每一个人才能发现或重新发现他最珍视的东西。于是我那诗人渴望创作的本能在胸中涌动，使我能让恐惧、怀疑，甚至绝望激发自己创作。在诗歌创作中，我觉得我和人类，和平凡的人紧密相连，他们坚守着自己的岗位，直到炸弹落下或是海浪席卷而来将他们淹没。坚守是因为他相信这是他能做得最好的事情，尽管这信仰难以用语言传达。但诗人比普通人幸运，因为他的工作始终是他的天职。确实，诗歌就像一种宗教使命，诗人甚至不再需要有宗教信仰，但因为诗歌或是不涉及琐事和转瞬即逝的事物，或是将它们作为本质和永恒的意象，所以诗歌至少是一种精神活动。

人需要有一种宗教信仰使

1 inarticulate /ˌɪnɑːˈtɪkjələt/ *adj.* 不善于表达的；词不达意的
2 transient /ˈtrænziənt/ *adj.* 短暂的
3 transmute /trænzˈmjuːt/ *v.* （使）变形

me something I didn't know I knew. So for me the compulsion of poetry is the sign of a belief, not the less real for being unformulated... a belief that men must enjoy life, explore life, enhance life. Each as best he can. And that I shall do these things best through the practice of poetry.

他的生活有意义。我希望我也能有这样的信仰，但我的任何信念总会充满困惑和保留看法。然而，我写诗就是努力发掘生活的意义。偶尔，我用诗歌表现自己的经历和感受，从中也明白了我不曾意识到自己却已经懂得的道理。因此，对我来说，诗歌创作的冲动表现出来的，不是因为不系统而不太真实的东西……而是一种信仰，那就是，人必须享受生活，探索生活的真谛，提高生活的品质。人可各尽其能。而我则通过写诗尽善尽美地完成我的使命。

含英咀华

本文是刘易斯给美国一个很著名的广播节目所写的一篇散文，在文中作者告诉读者人需要信仰的支撑，而作者的信仰就是履行一个诗人的职责，用诗歌来传递人间的真善美。文章首先引用叶芝的诗歌来点明当今的时代充满了信仰危机，然后笔锋一转，又告诉读者什么才是真正的信仰，最后作者说自己的信仰就是用诗歌来传递生活的真谛。

Francie Baltazar-Schwartz

弗朗西·巴尔塔萨-施瓦茨

弗朗西·巴尔塔萨-施瓦茨是一位美国餐饮业的大亨，同时又是美国一家著名的职业培训机构的顾问，写了很多有关职场法则和人生励志方面的小品文。

Attitude is Everything

Jerry was the kind of guy you love to hate. He was always in a good mood and always had something positive to say. When someone would ask him how he was doing, he would reply, "If I were any better, I would be twins!"

He was a unique[1] manager because he had several waiters who had followed him around from restaurant to restaurant. The reason the waiters followed Jerry was because of his attitude. He was a natural motivator[2]. If an employee was having a bad day, Jerry was there telling the employee how to look on the positive side of the situation.

Seeing this style really made me curious, so one day I went up to Jerry and asked him, "I don't get it! You can't be a positive person all of the time. How do you do it?" Jerry replied, "Each morning I wake up and say to myself, 'Jerry, you have two choices today. You can choose to be in a good mood or you can choose to be in a bad mood.' I choose to be in a good mood. Each time something bad happens, I can choose to be a victim[3] or I can choose to learn from it. I choose to learn from it. Every time someone comes to

1 unique /juːˈniːk/ adj. 独一无二的，独特的
2 motivator /ˈməʊtɪveɪtə/ n. 鼓动者
3 victim /ˈvɪktɪm/ n. 受害者

态度决定一切

杰瑞是那种你想要憎恨的人。他总是有好心情，并且讲一些积极的事情。当别人问他最近过得如何，他总是回答："如果我再过得好一些，我就比双胞胎还幸运啰！"

他是一位独特的经理，因为当他换工作的时候，许多服务生都跟着他从一家餐厅换到另一家。为什么呢？是源于他的态度。因为杰瑞是个天生的激励者，如果有某位员工今天运气不好，杰瑞总是适时地告诉那位员工往好的方面想。

看到这样的情景，真的让我很好奇，所以有一天我到杰瑞那儿问他："我不明白，没有人能够老是那样地积极乐观，你是怎么办到的？"杰瑞回答："每天早上我起来告诉自己：杰瑞，你今天有两种选择，你可以选择好心情，或者你可以选择坏心情。我选择好心情。即使有不好的事发生，我可以选择做个受害者，或是选择从中学习，我选择从中学习。每当有人跑来跟我抱怨，我可以选择接受抱怨或者指出

me complaining, I can choose to accept their complaining or I can point out the positive side of life. I choose the positive side of life."

"Yeah, right, it's not that easy," I protested.

"Yes it is," Jerry said. "Life is all about choices. When you cut away all the junk, every situation is a choice. You choose how you react to situations. You choose how people will affect your mood. You choose to be in a good mood or bad mood. The bottom line: it's your choice how you live life."

I reflected[1] on what Jerry said. Soon thereafter[2], I left the restaurant industry to start my own business. We lost touch, but often thought about him when I made a choice about life instead of reacting to it.

Several years later, I heard that Jerry did something you are never supposed to do in a restaurant business: he left the back door open one morning and was held up at gunpoint by three armed robbers. While trying to open the safe, his hand, shaking from nervousness, slipped off the combination. The robbers panicked and shot him. Luckily, Jerry was found relatively quickly and rushed to the local trauma center. After 18 hours of surgery and weeks of intensive care, Jerry was released from the hospital with fragments[3] of the bullets still in his body.

---

1 reflect /rɪˈflekt/　v.　反映
2 thereafter /ˌðeərˈɑːftə(r)/　adv.　其后，从那时以后
3 fragment /ˈfrægmənt/　n.　碎片，断片

生命光明的一面，我选择指出生命的光明一面。"

"但并不是每次都那么容易啊！"我反驳道。

"的确如此，"杰瑞说："生命就是一连串的选择，当你理清头绪时，每个状况都是一个选择，你选择如何响应，你选择人们如何影响你的心情，你选择处于好心情或是坏心情，说到底：你选择如何过你的生活。"

我思考着杰瑞所说的话。不久之后，我离开了餐饮业开创了自己的公司。我们失去了联系，但当我对生活做出一种选择而非对它做出反应时，我时常想起杰瑞。

数年后的一天，我听说杰瑞在一家餐饮企业做了一件你绝对想不到的事：有一天早上他没关餐厅的后门。结果，三个武装歹徒用枪劫持了他，他们要杰瑞打开保险箱，但由于过度紧张，杰瑞弄错了暗码，造成抢匪的惊慌，开枪射击了杰瑞。幸运的是，杰瑞比较及时地被发现，紧急送到医院抢救。经过十八个小时的外科手术以及精心的照顾，杰瑞终于出院了，但还有子弹碎片留在他

I saw Jerry about six months after the accident. When I asked him how he was, he replied, "If I were any better, I'd be twins. Wanna see my scars?"

I declined to see his wounds, but did ask him what had gone through his mind as the robbery took place. "The first thing that went through my mind was that I should have locked the back door," Jerry replied. "Then, as I lay on the floor, I remembered that I had two choices: I could choose to live, or I could choose to die. I chose to live."

"Weren't you scared? Did you lose consciousness?" I asked. Jerry continued, "The paramedics[1] were great. They kept telling me I was going to be fine. But when they wheeled me into the emergency room and I saw the expressions on the faces of the doctors and nurses, I got really scared. In their eyes, I read, 'He's a dead man.' I knew I needed to take action."

"What did you do?" I asked.

"Well, there was a big, burly[2] nurse shouting questions at me," said Jerry. "She asked if I was allergic to anything. 'Yes,' I replied. The doctors and nurses stopped working as they waited for my reply. I took a deep breath and yelled, 'Bullets!' Over their laughter, I told them, I am choosing to live.

---

1 paramedic /ˌpærəˈmedɪk/ *n.* 护理人员
2 burly /ˈbɜːli/ *adj.* 结实的，粗壮的

身上。

事件发生六个月之后，我遇到杰瑞，我问他最近怎么样。他回答："如果我再过得好一些，我就比双胞胎还幸运了。要看看我的伤痕吗？"

我婉拒了，但我问他当抢劫发生时，他的心路历程。杰瑞答道："我第一件想到的事情是我应该锁上后门的，当我躺在地板上时，还记得我有2个选择：我可以选择生，或选择死。我选择活下去。"

"你不害怕吗？你失去知觉了吗？"我问道。杰瑞继续说："医护人员真了不起。他们一直告诉我没事。但是当他们将我推入紧急手术间后，我看到医生跟护士脸上的神情，我真的被吓到了。从他们眼中，我看到：'他已经是个死人了。'我知道我需要采取行动。"

"当时你做了什么？"我问道。

杰瑞说："嗯！当时有个健壮的护士用吼叫的音量问我一个问题：她问我是否会对什么东西过敏。我回答："有，"这时医生跟护士都停下来等待我的回答。我深深地吸了一口气，接着喊，"子弹！"听他们笑完之后，我告诉他们："我现在选

Operate on me as if I am alive, not dead."

Jerry lived thanks to the skill of his doctors, but also because of his amazing attitude. I learned from him that every day we have the choice to live fully. Attitude, after all, is everything.

择活下去，请把我当做一个活生生的人来开刀，而不是一个活死人。"

杰瑞能活下去当然要归功于医生的精湛医术，但同时也由于他令人惊异的态度。我从他身上学到了每天我们都可以选择充实地生活。毕竟，态度决定一切。

含英咀华

在这篇文章中，作者用朴实的语言在向我们提出这样一个问题：我们怎样才能时刻保持乐观向上的精神呢?对大多数人而言，永恒的快乐似乎是可望而不可即的，但了不起的杰瑞独有其道。让我们分享他的秘诀,你会发现快乐和幽默不过是缘于一种选择，即以积极的态度对待身边的一切。永远积极面对人生，真的那么容易吗? 每一天，你都可以选择开心或是不开心；但是有一天，你必须去选择，是生，还是死，你发现只要你选择生存，你就一定可以，无论你将面临什么局面。正如在文章的结尾，作者所总结的那样：毕竟，态度决定一切。

海伦·海斯（1900～1993）在美国剧坛享有"第一夫人"的美誉，参演了多部百老汇电影、电视表演。她自五岁起就登台演出，九岁已演出百老汇舞台剧，十八岁就成为全国知名的明星。在她六十多年的演艺生涯中，曾三次获得托尼奖（Tony Award，世界上最著名和最大型的戏剧和音乐剧大奖）。她的电影作品1931年的《战地情天》(*The Sin of Madelon Claudet*) 和1970年的《机场》(*Airport*) 都获得了奥斯卡奖。

A Morning Prayer in a Little Church

小教堂里的晨祷

Once, years ago, I got into a dogfight. I was wheeling a baby carriage, my pet cocker spaniel[1] trotting[2] beside me. Without warning, three dogs — an Afghan, a St. Bernard and a Dalmatian — pounced on the cocker and started tearing him to pieces. I shrieked[3] for help. Two men in a car stopped, looked, and drove on.

When I saw that I was so infuriated[4] that I waded in[5] and stopped the fight myself. My theatrical training never stood me in better stead. My shouts were so authoritative, my gestures so arresting, I commanded the situation like a lion-tamer and the dogs finally slunk[6] away.

Looking back, I think I acted less in anger than from a realization that I was on my own, that if anybody was going to help me at that moment, it had to be myself.

Life seems to be a series of crises that have to be faced. In summoning strength to face them, though, I once fooled myself into

许多年以前，我曾经历过一场"狗狗大战"。当时我正推着婴儿车散步，我的狗（一只客卡猎犬）跟在我的左右。此时，不知从何而来的三只狗——一只阿富汗犬，一只圣伯纳和一只达尔马提亚犬——出其不意地向我的狗袭来！它们不停地攻击甚至于想把它撕成碎片。我大声呼救。两个开车的男人停了下来，旁观了一阵，接着又开走了。

我当时气急了！于是自己壮着胆子停止了那场"战役"。从前的戏剧训练带给了我极大的好处：不光是我的嗓音极具权威性，而且身体姿势也有震慑力——感觉上自己就像是一名驯狮者，那些狗狗们不得不灰溜溜地逃跑了。

现在回想起来，我想我表现得与其说愤怒还不如说是意识到了只有我自己一个人，如果当时没有任何人来帮助我的话，我就只能靠自己。

人生就是要面对一连串的波折。在鼓起勇气面对挫折的过

1　cocker spaniel /ˈkɒkə//ˈspænjəl/　n.　客卡猎犬
2　trot /trɒt/　v.　（马）小跑；快步走
3　shriek /ʃriːk/　v.　尖叫，叫喊
4　infuriated /ɪnˈfjuərieɪtɪd/　adj.　极为愤怒的
5　wade in　涉入（参与）；参加战斗。例如：Smith must wade in and delay the business with petty objections. （史密斯总是要来插手，用一些无关紧要的反对意见来耽误事情。）
6　slink（slunk, slunk）/slɪŋk/　v.　偷偷摸摸地走

an exaggerated[1] regard of my own importance. I felt very independent, I was only distantly aware of other people. I worked hard and was "successful". In the theater, I was brought up in the tradition of service. The audience pays its money and I am expected to give my best performance — both on and off the stage. So I served on committees, and made speeches, and backed causes. But somehow the meaning of things escaped me.

When my daughter died of polio[2], everybody stretched out a hand to help me, but at first I couldn't seem to bear the touch of anything, even the love of friends; no support seemed strong enough.

While Mary was still sick, I used to go early in the morning to a little church near the hospital to pray. There the working people came quietly to worship. I had been careless with my religion. I had rather cut God out of my life, and I didn't have the nerve at the time to ask Him to make my daughter well — I only asked Him to help me understand, to let me come in and reach Him. I prayed there every morning and I kept looking for a revelation[3], but nothing happened.

And then, much later, I discovered that it had happened, right there in the church. I could recall, vividly, one by one, the people I had seen there — the solemn[4] laborers with tired

程中，我曾一度自我感觉过于良好。我觉得自己相当独立，并和别人保持距离感。我十分努力地工作，也相当"成功"。在剧院，我得到了一个好演员应得的传统好待遇。观众们花钱来看我演戏，所以我就尽最大努力演好我的戏——不论是台上还是台下。所以我担当委员会的委员，四处发表演说，然后得到成功的事业。但是，不知为何，我感到生活空虚极了。

当我的女儿玛莉因小儿麻痹症去世后，人人都伸出援手想帮我。但是一开始我甚至不敢去接受任何人的帮助，就算是朋友们的爱，仿佛没有一种力量足够强大到救我脱离苦海。

当玛莉还躺在病床上时，我常常每天早晨去医院附近的一所小教堂祈祷。那儿是劳动人民每天都会安静地做祷告的地方。我曾对自己的宗教信仰很不在意。甚至一度把上帝从我的生命中忽略掉，所以那时我并没有勇气祈求他让我的女儿康复——而是请他帮我理解，让我能够更接近他。每天早晨我都会去祈祷，并寻求启示，但是什么都没有改变。

很久以后，我才发现，改

1 exaggerated /ɪgˈzædʒəreɪtɪd/ *adj.* 夸大的，夸张的，言过其实的
2 polio /ˈpəʊliəʊ/ *n.* <口语>小儿麻痹症
3 revelation /ˌrevəˈleɪʃn/ *n.* 透露，显示，启示；新发现
4 solemn /ˈsɒləm/ *adj.* 庄严的，隆重的；严肃的

looks, the old women with gnarled[1] hands. Life had knocked them around, but for a brief moment they were being refreshed by an ennobling experience. It seemed as they prayed their worn faces lighted up and they became the very vessels[2] of God. Here was my revelation. Suddenly I realized I was one of them. In my need I gained strength from the knowledge that they too had needs, and I felt an interdependence with them. I experienced a flood of compassion[3] for people. I was learning the meaning of "love thy neighbor".

Truths as old and simple as this began to light up for me like the faces of the men and women in the little church. When I read the Bible[4] now, as I do frequently, I take the teachings of men like Jesus and David and St. Paul as the helpful advice of trusted friends about how to live. They understand that life is full of complications and often heavy blows and they are showing me the wisest way through it. I must help myself, yes, but I am not such a self-contained unit that I can live aloof[5], unto myself. This was the meaning that had been missing before: the realization that I was a living part of God's world of people.

1 gnarled /nɑːld/ adj. （树木）多节的，粗糙的
2 vessel /ˈvesl/ n. 导管，血管
3 compassion /kəmˈpæʃn/ n. 怜悯；同情
4 Bible /ˈbaɪbl/ n. 圣经
5 aloof /əˈluːf/ adv. 远离，离开

变的确发生了，就在那个小教堂里。我能清楚地回忆起在那儿我所见过的每一个人——面带倦容的工人们和手指粗糙多节的老妇人们。生活让他们不得不辛苦劳作，但是在这一刻他们的生命被崇高的经历重新注入了力量。祈祷过后，他们疲惫的面容一下子被点亮了，仿佛他们也成了上帝的一个重要部分。这就是我得到的启示：突然间我意识到自己也是他们的一分子。为了满足需要，我会不断从知识中吸取力量，他们也是。我感到原来我们大家都是相互依赖，彼此共生的。那时一股强烈的对人们的同情怜悯之感油然而生。我真正领悟到了"爱邻如爱己"的真谛。

古老而又简明的真理就如同点亮了小教堂里那些男男女女的生命般，也点亮了我的生命。现在每当我读圣经的时候，我时常都会将耶稣，大卫以及圣保罗的关于怎样去生活的建议当做是我最信赖朋友的忠告。他们知道生命充满了复杂的状况和各种各样的挫折，并教导我用最明智的方法去面对挫折。自救是没错，不过我肯定不是一个远离人群独自生活的个体。这就是之前被我忽略了许久的真理：我是上帝创造的人类世界中的一员。

含英咀华

　　本文作者通过自己的经历，采取夹叙夹议的方式阐明主题：人需要努力去生活，但是作为个体，人也需要融入社会这个整体中去。即使面对挫折时，你能采取自己的方式调整自己，也不要让自己成为"一个远离人群独自生活的个体"，因为作为这个社会的一分子，人与人应该相互依赖，共同生存。

Ernest Hemingway
厄内斯特·海明威

厄尼斯特·海明威(1899~1961)，美国著名小说家，1954年获诺贝尔文学奖。四十年代出版成名作《太阳照样升起》(*The Sun Also Rises, 1926*)，被称为"迷惘的一代"(*the Lost Generation*)代表作。短篇小说集《没有女人的男人》(*Men Without Women , 1927*)和《胜者无所得》(*Winner Take Nothing, 1933*)确立了他短篇小说大师的地位。《永别了，武器》(*A Farewell to Arms, 1929*)、《丧钟为谁而鸣》(*For Whom the Bell Tolls, 1940*)这两部反战长篇小说被誉为现代世界文学名著。中篇小说《老人与海》(*The Old Man and the Sea, 1952*)获得普利策奖。1932年发表了《午后之死》(*Death in the Afternoon*)，提出了"冰山原则"(*the Iceberg Principle*)，即只表现事物的八分之一，使作品充实、含蓄、耐人寻味。

True Nobility

In a calm sea, every man is a pilot.

But all sunshine without shade, all pleasure without pain, is not life at all. Take the lot of the happiest—it is a tangled[1] yarn. Bereavements[2] and blessings, one following another, make us sad and blessed by turns. Even death itself makes life more loving. Men come closest to their true selves in the sober[3] moments of life, under the shadows of sorrow and loss.

In the affairs of life or of business, it is not intellect that tells so much as character, not brains so much as heart, not genius so much as self-control, patience, and discipline, regulated by judgment.

I have always believed that the man who has begun to live more seriously within begins to live more simply without. In an age of extravagance[4] and waste, I wish I could show to the world how few the real wants of humanity are.

To regret one's errors to the point of not repeating them is true repentance. There is nothing noble in being superior to some other

1 tangled /'tæŋgld/   adj.   复杂的
2 bereavement /bɪ'riːvmənt/   n.   丧亲之痛
3 sober /'səʊbə/   adj.   清醒的
4 extravagance /ɪk'strævəgəns/   n.   奢侈, 铺张, 过度, 放纵的言行

真实的高贵

在风平浪静的大海上，每个人都是领航员。

但是，只有阳光而无阴影，只有欢乐而无痛苦，那就不是人生。以最幸福的人的生活为例——它是一团纠缠在一起的纱线。丧亲之痛和幸福祝愿，彼此相接，使我们一会儿伤心，一会儿高兴。甚至死亡本身也会使生命更加可亲。在人生的清醒时刻，在哀痛和伤心的阴影之下，人类与真实的自我最接近。

在生活或事业中，性格比才智更能指导我们，心灵比头脑更能引导我们，而由判断而得的克制、耐心和教养比天分更能让我们受益。

我一向认为，内心开始生活得更为严谨的人，他外在的生活会开始变得更为简朴。在物欲横流的年代，但愿我能向世人表明：人类的真正需求少得多么可怜。

悔恨自己的错误，而且力求不再重蹈覆辙，这才是真正的悔悟。优于别人，并不高

man. The true nobility is in being superior to your previous[1] self.

贵。真正的高贵应该是优于过去的自己。

---

1 previous /'pri:vɪəs/   *adj.*   事前的；以前的

含英咀华

　　《真实的高贵》这篇优美的散文，以简约、清新的风格表现作者努力超越自己的执著。也许人生最大的满足应该是来自对目标的追求，但人一旦在自己所从事的领域达到巅峰时，就会有一种接踵而至的空前的寂寞——发现成功后的自己再也无法超越已经获得的成功，所以如何超越自己是一个值得深思的话题。

Orison Marden

奥里森·马登

本文作者简介见《让心中充满阳光》。

The Man and the Opportunity

人与机遇

The lack of opportunity is ever the excuse of a weak, vacillating[1] mind. Opportunities! Every life is full of them.

Every lesson in school or college is an opportunity. Every examination is a chance in life. Every business transaction[2] is an opportunity — an opportunity to be polite, an opportunity to be manly, an opportunity to be honest, an opportunity to make friends. Every proof of confidence in you is a great opportunity. Every responsibility thrusts[3] upon your strength and your honor is priceless. Existence is the privilege of effort and when that privilege is met like a man, opportunities to succeed along the line of your aptitude[4] will come faster than you can use them.

Young men and women, why do you stand here all the day idle? Was the land all occupied before you were born? Has the earth ceased to yield its increase? Are the seats all taken? The positions all filled? The chances all gone? Are the resources of your country fully developed? Are the secrets of nature all mastered? Is

缺乏机遇一向是意志薄弱、遇事踌躇者的借口。机遇！每一个人的一生都充满着机遇！

在学院或者大学的每一堂课都是一次机遇。每一次考试都是人生中的一次契机。每一次商业交易都是一次机会———次以礼待人的机会，一次展示男子汉气概的机会，一次以诚相见的机会、一次交到朋友的机会。每次对你信心的考验就是一个莫大的机会。每一种加在你的能力与荣誉上的责任都是无价的。生存是努力赋予的特权，我们邂逅这种特权就像偶然遇到某个人一样，机遇会随着你的能力接踵而至，甚至让你应接不暇。

年轻的小伙子们和姑娘们，为什么你们整天懒散地站在这里呢？难道在你们出生之前，土地就已经被占据一空了吗？难道地球就已经不再繁衍生息了吗？难道所有的位置都已经坐满，所有的职务都没有

1 vacillate /'væsəleɪt/ v. 犹豫不定，踌躇不决
2 transaction /træn'zækʃn/ n. 交易，事务
3 thrust /θrʌst/ v. 插入，将……强加于
4 aptitude /'æptɪtjuːd/ n. 天资，才能

there no way in which you can utilize[1] these passing moments to improve yourself or benefit another?

Don't wait for your opportunity. Make it, make it as Napoleon made his in a hundred "impossible" situations. Make it, as all leaders of men, in war and in peace, have made their chances of success. Make it, as every man must, who would accomplish anything worth the effort. Golden opportunities are nothing to laziness, but industry makes the commonest chances golden.

空缺了吗？难道机会都跑光了吗？难道你们国家所有的资源都已经开发殆尽了吗？自然界的奥秘你们都完全掌握了吗？难道你们无法抓住这稍纵即逝的时光去改造自己或造福他人吗？

切莫坐等良机。创造机会，就像拿破仑在无数次"绝境"中创造机会一样。创造机会，就像所有战争或和平时期的领袖创造他们成功的机会那样。创造机会，如果你想努力成就一番事业，就必须这么做。对于懒人来说，即使上天赐给他再好的机会他也会一无所获；而勤奋的人却能通过最微小的机会创造出辉煌。

---

1 utilize /'juːtəlaɪz/ *v.* 利用

含英咀华

　　这篇文章以积极乐观的态度鼓励人们把握机会，创造机会。即使是一次上课，一次考试，一次商业交易都是人生中一次珍贵的机遇。文章虽短，却通过"难道……难道……"这样的排比句式不断加强语言的感染力，透过这些充满激情的文字，作者把自己的信心和士气传递给了读者。

Helen Keller

海伦·凯勒

本文作者简介见《假如给我三天光明》。

The Light of a Brighter Day

更光明的未来

I choose for my subject faith wrought into life apart from[1] creed or dogma[2]. By faith, I mean a vision of good one cherishes and the enthusiasm that pushes one to seek its fulfillment, regardless of[3] obstacles. Faith is a dynamic power that breaks the chain of routine, and gives a new, fine turn to old commonplaces. Faith reinvigorates[4] the will, enriches the affections, and awakens a sense of creativeness. Active faith knows no fear, and it is a safeguard to me against cynicism[5] and despair.

After all, faith is not one thing or two or three things. It is an indivisible totality of beliefs that inspire me: Belief in God as infinite goodwill and all-seeing wisdom, whose everlasting arms sustain me walking on the sea of life. Trust in my fellow men, wonder at their fundamental goodness, and confidence that after this night of sorrow and oppression, they will rise up strongly and beautifully in the glory of morning. Reverence for the beauty and preciousness of the earth,

我选择生活信仰，而不是教义或信条，作为我的主题。在我看来，信仰是指一个人拥有的美好梦想，以及激励他无论遇到什么困难都要实现梦想的热情。信仰是一种充满生机的力量，它能冲破常规的束缚，使平淡无奇的事物焕发新的光彩。信仰能重新激发人的意志，丰富人的情感并唤醒人的创造力。积极的信仰无所畏惧，对我来说，它能使我不至愤世嫉俗，陷入绝境。

归根结底，信仰并不只是一两种具体的表现，而是鼓励着我的无数信念构成的不可分割的整体：相信上帝具有无穷无尽的善意和全知的智慧，他永恒的翅膀支撑着我在生活的海洋中前行。信任我的同伴，为他们本性的善良和信心所折服，因为他们相信在经历了这个充满悲伤和压迫的漫漫长夜之后，他们将坚强地站起来，成为晨光中一道美丽的风景。对地球上的美丽和珍贵的事物充满敬畏，觉得自己有责任尽

1 apart from   除……之外。例如：Apart from the injuries to his face and hands, he broke both legs. （他不仅脸上和手上伤痕累累，两条腿也摔断了。）
2 dogma /ˈdɒɡmə/ n. 教条
3 regardless of   不顾，不惜。例如：They decorated the house regardless of cost. （他们不惜工本装修这栋房子。）
4 reinvigorate /ˌriːɪnˈvɪɡəreɪt/ v. 使再振作，使复生
5 cynicism /ˈsɪnɪsɪzəm/ n. 愤世嫉俗

and a sense of responsibility to do what I can to make it a habitation of health and plenty for all men. Faith in immortality because it renders less bitter the separation from those I have loved and lost, and because it will free me from unnatural limitations, and unfold still more faculties I have in joyous activity.

Even if my vital spark should be blown out, I believe that I should behave with courageous dignity in the presence of fate, and strive to be a worthy companion of the beautiful, the good, and the true. But fate has its master in the faith of those who surmount[1] it, and limitation has its limits for those who, though disillusioned, live greatly.

It was a terrible blow to my faith when I learned that millions of my fellow creatures must labor all their days for food and shelter, bear the most crushing burdens, and die without having known the joy of living. My security vanished[2] forever, and I have never regained the radiant belief of my young years that earth is a happy home and hearth for the majority of mankind. But faith is a state of mind. The believer is not soon disheartened. If he is turned out of his shelter, he builds up a house that the winds of the earth can not destroy.

When I think of the suffering and famine, and the continued slaughter[3] of men, my spirit

---

1 surmount /səˈmaʊnt/   v. 克服，越过
2 vanish /ˈvænɪʃ/ v. 消失
3 slaughter /ˈslɔːtə(r)/   n. 残杀，屠杀

我所能使地球成为全人类健康而富庶的家园。相信永恒，因为这种信仰能使我与我深爱着的但却失去的人分离时不至于悲痛欲绝，因为它能使我摆脱人为的限制，发觉自己也有享受快乐的能力。

即使我的生命之光终将熄灭，我相信在命运前，我将勇敢面对，保持尊严，努力抗争，与真善美相伴。但是命运也掌握着那些战胜命运者的信仰，限制也不能完全剥夺理想破灭的人勇敢生活的权利。

当我知道我的无数同伴为了维持生计必须终日劳作，背负着最沉重的负担，还没有来得及品尝生命的快乐就黯然离去，我的信仰遭受了沉重打击。我的安全感完全消失了，我从此失去了年少时曾拥有的让人喜悦的信念：地球是大多数人幸福生活的家园。但信仰是一种精神状态。有信仰的人从不轻易气馁。如果他被迫流离失所，他会重新修建一所地球上的任何风都无法摧毁的房子。

想到正在承受着苦难和饥荒的人们，想到人类无休止地相互杀戮，我的心灵就会流血，但我的脑海里突然出现了

bleeds. But the thought comes to me that, like the little deaf, dumb and blind child I once was, mankind is growing out of the darkness of ignorance and hate into the light of a brighter day.

一个念头：就像我曾是一个失明的聋哑孩子时那样，人类正渐渐从无知和仇恨的黑暗中成长起来，走向更光明的未来。

含英咀华

在这篇文章中，海伦告诉读者信仰的力量，以及要接受生命的挑战，用爱心去拥抱世界，要像她那样以惊人的毅力面对困境，在黑暗中找到光明，把慈爱的双手伸向全世界。在这个充满信仰危机的时代，本文就像一把火炬，为在黑暗中前行的人们指明了道路。

Steve Jobs

史蒂夫·乔布斯

史蒂夫·乔布斯（1955~2011），苹果电脑公司（*Apple Computer*）的创始人，苹果电脑公司和皮克斯动画公司（*Pixar Animation Studios*）首席执行官。史蒂夫出生以及成长于硅谷。1972年高中毕业后，他在波兰的一所大学中只念了一学期的书。1976年，年仅21岁的乔布斯和26岁的沃兹尼艾克在乔布斯家的车库里成立了苹果电脑公司。其后，苹果电脑成为美国最成功的电脑公司。不过在1985年，他也被自己请回来的CEO扫地出门。乔布斯总能找到开发新产品的技术。1997年，乔布斯重返苹果成为CEO，次年他就推出了美国当年最畅销个人电脑iMac。而其后的iPod音乐播放器，再次让苹果成为世界上最成功的公司之一。

Stay Hungry, Stay Foolish

I am honored to be with you today at your commencement[1] from one of the finest universities in the world. I never graduated from college. Truth be told, this is the closest I've ever gotten to a college graduation.

When I was 17, I read a quote that went something like: "If you live each day as if it was your last, someday you'll most certainly be right." It made an impression on me, and since then, for the past 33 years, I have looked in the mirror every morning and asked myself: "If today were the last day of my life, would I want to do what I am about to do today?" And whenever the answer has been "No" for too many days in a row, I know I need to change something.

Remembering that I'll be dead soon is the most important tool I've ever encountered to help me make the big choices in life. Because almost everything — all external expectations, all pride, all fear of embarrassment or failure — these things just fall away in the face of death, leaving only what is truly important. Remembering that you are going to die is the best way I know to

---

1 commencement /kə'mensmənt/ n. 开始；毕业典礼

求知若饥，
虚心若愚

很荣幸和大家一道参加这所世界上最好的大学之一的毕业典礼。对于我这个大学没有毕业的人而言，说实话，这是我离大学毕业典礼最近的一刻。

在我17岁那年，我读到过这样一段话，大意是："如果把每一天都当做生命的最后一天，总有一天你会活得轻松自在。"我记住了这句话，从那时起，33年过去了，我每天早晨都对着镜子自问："假如今天是生命的最后一天，我还会去做今天要做的事吗？"如果连续几天我的回答都是"不"，我知道自己应该有所改变了。

让我能够做出人生重大抉择的最主要方法是，记住生命随时都有可能结束。因为几乎所有的东西——所有对自身之外的需求、所有的尊严、所有对困窘以及失败的恐惧——在面对死亡时都将不复存在，只剩下真正有价值的东西。记住自己随时都会死去，这是我所知道的防止患得患失的最有效

avoid the trap of thinking you have something to lose. You are already naked. There is no reason not to follow your heart.

About a year ago I was diagnosed with cancer. I had a scan[1] at 7:30 in the morning, and it clearly showed a tumor[2] on my pancreas[3]. I didn't even know what a pancreas was. The doctors told me this was almost certainly a type of cancer that is incurable, and that I should expect to live no longer than three to six months. My doctor advised me to go home and get my affairs in order, which is doctor's code for preparing to die. It means to try to tell your kids everything you thought you'd have the next 10 years to tell them in just a few months. It means to make sure everything is buttoned up[4] so that it will be as easy as possible for your family. It means to say your goodbyes.

I lived with that diagnosis[5] all day. Later that evening I had a biopsy[6], where they stuck an endoscope[7] down my throat, through my stomach and into my intestines[8], put a needle into my pancreas and got a few cells from the tumor. I was sedated[9], but my wife, who was there, told me that when they viewed the cells under a

途径。你已经一无所有了。还有什么理由不跟着自己的感觉走呢。

大约一年前，我被诊断患了癌症。那天早上七点半，我做了一次扫描检查，结果清楚地表明我的胰腺上长了一个肿瘤，可那时我连胰腺是什么还不知道呢！医生告诉我说，几乎可以确诊这是一种无法治愈的恶性肿瘤，我最多还能活 3 到 6 个月。医生建议我回去把一切都安排好，其实这是在暗示"准备后事"。也就是说，把今后十年要跟孩子们说的事情在这几个月内嘱咐完；也就是说，把一切都安排妥当，尽可能不给家人留麻烦；也就是说，去跟大家诀别。

那一整天里，我的脑子一直想着这个诊断。到了晚上，我做了一次组织切片检查，他们把一个内窥镜通过喉咙穿过我的胃进入肠子，用针头从胰腺的瘤子上取了一些细胞组织。当时我被麻醉了，陪在一旁的妻子后来告诉我，医生在显微镜里看了细胞之后叫了起来，原来这是一种少见的可以通过外科手术治愈的恶性肿瘤。我做了手术，现在好了。

这是我和死神离得最近的

---

1 scan /skæn/　*n.*　扫描，细查
2 tumor /'tjuːmə(r)/　*n.*　肿块
3 pancreas /'pæŋkriəs/　*n.*　胰腺
4 button up　完成，确定。例如：Let's button up the job.（让我们把
　　　　　　　这活干完吧。）
5 diagnosis /ˌdaɪəg'nəʊsɪs/　*n.*　诊断
6 biopsy /'baɪɒpsi/　*n.*　[医]活组织检查，活组织切片检查，
　　　　　　　活体检查
7 endoscope /'endəskəʊp/　*n.*　内窥镜
8 intestine /ɪn'testɪn/　*n.*　肠
9 sedate /sɪ'deɪt/　*v.*　给……服镇静剂

microscope the doctors started crying because it turned out to be a very rare form of pancreatic[1] cancer that is curable with surgery. I had the surgery and I'm fine now.

This was the closest I've been to facing death, and I hope it's the closest I get for a few more decades. Having lived through it, I can now say this to you with a bit more certainty than when death was a useful but purely intellectual concept.

No one wants to die. Even people who want to go to heaven don't want to die to get there. And yet death is the destination we all share. No one has ever escaped it. And that is as it should be, because Death is very likely the single best invention of Life. It is Life's change agent. It clears out the old to make way for the new. Right now the new is you, but someday not too long from now, you will gradually become the old and be cleared away. Sorry to be so dramatic, but it is quite true.

Your time is limited, so don't waste it living someone else's life. Don't be trapped by dogma — which is living with the results of other people's thinking. Don't let the noise of other's opinions drown out your own inner voice. And most important, have the courage to follow your heart and intuition[2]. They somehow already know what you truly want to become. Everything else is secondary.

---

1 pancreatic /ˌpæŋkriˈætɪk/ *adj.* 胰腺的
2 intuition /ˌɪntjuˈɪʃn/ *n.* 直觉，直觉的知识

一次，我希望也是今后几十年里最近的一次。有了这次经历之后，现在我可以更加确切地和你们谈论死亡，而不是纯粹纸上谈兵。

没有人愿意死。即使是那些想进天堂的人，他们也希望能够活着进天堂。然而，死亡是所有人的归宿，没人能够幸免。我们注定会死，因为死亡很可能是生命最伟大的一项发明。它是生命得以延续的媒介。老者逝去，为新生儿留出空间。现在，你们就是新生儿，但在不久的将来，你们也会逐渐成为老人，也会被淘汰出人生的舞台。对不起，我把话说得如此戏剧化，不过这是千真万确的。

你们的时间是有限的，所以不要浪费时间去按照别人的意愿活着。不要囿于成见——那是在按照别人设想的结果而活。不要让他人观点的聒噪声淹没自己的心声。最主要的是，要有跟着自己感觉和直觉走的勇气。无论如何，心灵和直觉早就知道你到底想成为什么样的人。其他都是次要的。

我年轻时有一本非常好的刊物，叫《全球概览》，这是我那代人的宝书之一。创办人名叫斯图尔特·布兰德，就住

When I was young, there was an amazing publication called The Whole Earth Catalog[1], which was one of the bibles of my generation. It was created by a fellow named Stewart Brand not far from here in Menlo Park, and he brought it to life with his poetic touch. This was in the late 1960's, before personal computers and desktop publishing, so it was all made with typewriters, scissors, and polaroid[2] cameras. It was sort of like Google in paperback form, 35 years before Google came along: it was idealistic, and overflowing[3] with neat tools and great notions.

Stewart and his team put out several issues of The Whole Earth Catalog, and then when it had run its course, they put out a final issue. It was the mid-1970s, and I was your age. On the back cover of their final issue was a photograph of an early morning country road, the kind you might find yourself hitchhiking[4] on if you were so adventurous. Beneath it were the words: "Stay Hungry. Stay Foolish." It was their farewell[5] message as they signed off. Stay Hungry. Stay Foolish. And I have always wished that for myself. And now, as you graduate to begin anew, I wish that for you.

Stay Hungry. Stay Foolish.

Thank you all very much.

在离这儿不远的门洛帕克市。他用诗一般的语言把刊物办得很有活力。那是20世纪60年代末，还没有个人电脑和桌面印刷系统，一切全靠打字机、剪刀和拍立得照相机。它就像一种纸质的谷歌，却比谷歌早问世了35年。这份刊物十分完美，它的查阅手段齐备、构思不凡。

斯图尔特和他的同事们出了好几期《全球概览》，到最后办不下去时，他们出了最后一期。那是20世纪70年代中期，我也就是你们现在的年纪。停刊号的封底是一张清晨乡间小路的照片，那种你搭便车做探险旅行时会经过的乡间小路。照片下面写道：求知若饥，虚心若愚。那是他们停刊前的告别词。求知若饥，虚心若愚。这也是我一直想做到的。现在，在你们即将离开校园、开始新的生活的时候，我也以此来期许你们：

求知若饥，虚心若愚。
谢谢大家。

1 catalog /ˈkætəlɒg/　n.　目录，大学概况手册
2 polaroid /ˈpəʊlərɔɪd/　拍立得照相机（美国拍立得公司1947年制成，照相曝光60秒即可取得相片）（= Polaroid camera）（商标名称）
3 overflow /ˌəʊvəˈfləʊ/　使溢出；使泛滥
4 hitchhike /ˈhɪtʃhaɪk/　v.　搭便车
5 farewell /ˌfeəˈwel/　n.　告别

含英咀华

本文节选自乔布斯2005年6月在斯坦福大学的演讲，他在演讲中讲了三个故事。第一个故事讲述人生中的点点滴滴如何串在一起；第二个故事讲述好恶与得失；本文选取的是第三个故事，关于死亡的故事。他给我们讲述了他成功的秘诀，那就是把每一天都当做人生的最后一天。这样，你就会认真地安排又安排，让时间得到最大限度的利用，同时也没有时间去体验烦恼、无聊等种种情绪。如果能够一直保持这样的心态，那么成功就是自然而然的事了。

Richard Carlson
理查德·卡尔森

理查德·卡尔森(1961~2006)，美国著名的教育专家，知名的演说家和心理咨询专家，著有全球畅销书《找回喜悦的心》(*You Can Feel Good Again, 1994*)、《别为小事抓狂》(*Don't Sweat the Small Stuff…and It's All Small Stuff, 1997*)系列、《放慢生活的速度》(*Slowing Down to the Speed of Life, 1997*)等。卡尔森以轻松温馨的文笔，提供各种简单有效的生活与工作智慧，帮助大家用宽容自在的心情开创和谐人生。他的演说和著作风靡全世界，已成为新时代的激励大师。他曾被《人物》(*People*)称为"最有魅力的人"，曾多次受邀参加《奥普拉脱口秀》(*The Oprah Winfrey Show*)等知名谈话节目，接受CNN等专访，鼓励人们将他书中所提倡的观念落实到日常生活中。

Surrender to the Fact that Life Isn't Fair

承认生活不公平这一事实

A friend of mine, in response to a conversation we were having about the injustices of life, asked me the question, "Who said life was going to be fair, or that it was even meant to be fair?" Her question was a good one. It reminded me of something I was taught as a youngster: Life isn't fair. It's a bummer[1], but it's absolutely true. One of the mistakes many of us make is that we feel sorry for ourselves, or for others, thinking that life should be fair, or that some day it will be. It's not and it won't.

One of the nice things about surrendering to the fact that life isn't fair is that it keeps us from feeling sorry for ourselves by encouraging us to do the very best we can with what we have. We know it's not "life's job" to make everything perfect, it's our own challenge. Surrendering to this fact also keeps us from feeling sorry for others because we are reminded that everyone is dealt a different hand; everyone has unique strengths and problems in the process of growing up, facing the reality and making decisions; and everyone has those times that they feel victimized

一位友人就生活的不公平交谈时，她问了我这样一个问题，"谁说生活会是公平的，或生活应该是公平的？"这个问题问得好。它让我想起年轻时汲取的一个教训：生活是不公平的。这着实让人不愉快，但的确是实情。我们许多人所犯的一个错误便是为自己、或为他人感到遗憾，认为生活应该是公平的，或者终会有一天会是公平的。其实不然，现在不是，将来也不会。

承认生活并不公平这一事实的一个好处便是它激励我们去尽己所能，而不再自我感伤。我们知道让每件事情完美并不是"生活的使命"，而是我们自己对生活的挑战。承认这一事实也会让我们不再为他人遗憾，因为我们领悟到每个人都被分与一副不同的牌；每个人在成长、面对现实、做种种决定的过程中都有各自不同的能力和难题，每个人都有感到成了牺牲品或遭受不公正对

---

1 bummer /'bʌmə(r)/ *n.* 令人不愉快的事物

or unfairly treated.

The fact that life isn't fair doesn't mean we shouldn't do everything in our power to improve our own lives or the world as a whole. To the contrary, it suggests that we should. When we don't recognize or admit that life isn't fair, we tend to feel pity for others and for ourselves. Pity, of course, is a self-defeating emotion that does nothing for anyone, except to make everyone feel worse than they already do. When we do recognize that life isn't fair, however, we feel compassion for others and for ourselves. And compassion is heartfelt[1] emotions that delivers loving kindness to everyone it touches. The next time you find yourself thinking about the injustices of the world, try reminding yourself of this very basic fact. You may be surprised that it can nudge[2] you out of self-pity and into helpful action.

待的时候。

承认生活并不公平这一事实并不意味我们不必尽己所能去改善生活，去改进整个世界。恰恰相反，它正表明我们应该这样做。当我们没有意识到或不承认生活并不公平时，我们往往怜悯他人也怜悯自己。怜悯自然是一种于任何人无补的有违初衷的情绪，它只能令人感觉比现在更糟。但当我们真正意识到生活并不公平时，我们会对他人也对自己怀有同情。同情是一种由衷的情感，所到之处都会散发出充满爱意的仁慈。以后等你发现自己在思考世界上的种种不公正时，可要提醒自己这一基本的事实。你或许会惊奇地发现它会将你从自我怜悯中拉出来，推动你采取一些具有积极意义的行动。

---

1 **heartfelt** /ˈhɑːtfelt/   *adj.*   衷心的，真心真意的
2 **nudge** /nʌdʒ/   *n./v.*   （用肘）轻推

含英咀华

在本文中，作者告诉大家承认生活不公平这一事实，并不是把它当做悲观消极的借口，相反，这样能帮助人们走出悲天悯人的阴影，以一种积极的人生态度迎接挑战。每个人的能力与经历迥异，得到的结果也不尽相同，但是命运赋予每个人选择生活的权利是一样的。一个人面对社会不公的事实，是选择逃避，就此沉沦，还是心怀感念，积极入世，关键还要看个人的修养和心态，以及对人生的参悟。

一叶知秋
脚踏实地

Walter Whitman
华尔特·惠特曼

华尔特·惠特曼（1819~1892），美国浪漫主义最伟大的诗人和杰出的民主诗人。他一生创作了大量诗歌，编入《草叶集》(Leaves of Grass, 1855)。在艺术上，惠特曼打破传统的诗歌格律，创造了"自由体"(free verse)的形式，借以充分地表达自己的思想感情。惠特曼的创作分三个时期。南北战争前，他的诗歌主要是反对奴隶制和民族压迫，歌颂自由和民主；南北战争期间，他激励人们投入反奴隶制战争，歌颂战争英雄，哀悼被刺的林肯总统；战后，惠特曼的诗歌讴歌欧洲革命运动，赞颂人类物质文明。

The Lesson of a Tree

I SHOULD not take either the biggest or the most picturesque tree to illustrate it. Here is one of my favorites now before me, a fine yellow poplar, quite straight, perhaps 90 feet high, and four thick at the butt. How strong, vital, enduring! How dumbly eloquent[1]! What suggestions of imperturbability[2] and being, as against the human trait of mere seeming[3]. Then the qualities, almost emotional, palpably[4] artistic, heroic, of a tree; so innocent and harmless, yet so savage. It is, yet says nothing. How it rebukes by its tough and equable serenity all weathers, this gusty-temper'd little whiffet[5], man that runs indoors at a mite of rain or snow. Science (or rather half-way science) scoffs[6] at reminiscence of dryad and hamadryad, and of trees speaking. But, if they don't, they do as well as most speaking, writing, poetry, sermons—or rather they do a great deal better. I should say indeed that those old dryad-reminiscences are quite as true as any, and profounder than most reminiscences we get. ("Cut this out," as the quack mediciners say, and keep

---

1 eloquent /ˈeləkwənt/ adj. 雄辩的，有口才的，动人的
2 imperturbability /ˌɪmpəˈtɜːbəˈbɪləti/ n. 沉着冷静
3 the human trait of mere seeming 人生的浮华表现
4 palpably /ˈpælpəbli/ adv. 可触摸地，明显地
5 gusty-temper'd little whiffet 无用的小东西
6 scoff /skɒf/ v. 讽刺，嘲笑

一棵树的启示

我不会列举最直耸云天或最绚烂夺目的树来说明这个问题。现在我面前的是一棵我最爱的树，一棵茂盛的黄白杨，树干笔直，可能有九十英尺高，最粗的地方有四英尺粗。多么强壮，多么生机勃勃，多么坚忍不拔！多么口若悬河，而又默默无闻！这是沉着冷静，存在即真的表现，与人仅仅注重外表的性格恰恰相反。一棵树情感丰富，艺术感唾手可得，英雄气十足；天真无知，无心害人，而又冷酷无情。一棵树具备这些气质，却从不言语。树以坚强和一如既往的平静指责所有雨雪阴晴的天气，大风袭来也只是轻轻摇曳，只要有一丝雨水或一片雪花，人们就会跑进室内。科学（或伪科学）嘲笑人们回忆森林女神和树神，消耗小树间的轻语。但是，如果他们不介意，他们同样可以讲演，可以写作，可以吟诗，可以布道——或者他们可以做得更好。我应该说这些古老的回忆

by you.) Go and sit in a grove or woods, with one or more of those voiceless companions, and read the foregoing, and think.

One lesson from affiliating[1] a tree—perhaps the greatest moral lesson anyhow from earth, rocks, animals, is that same lesson of inherency, of what is, without the least regard to what the looker on (the critic) supposes or says, or whether he likes or dislikes. What worse—what more general malady[2] pervades each and all of us, our literature, education, attitude toward each other, (even toward ourselves,) than a morbid trouble about seems, (generally temporarily seems too,) and no trouble at all, or hardly any, about the sane, slow-growing, perennial[3], real parts of character, books, friendship, marriage—humanity's invisible foundations and hold-together?

的确千真万确，比我们所作的大多数追忆更加深刻。（"把树切断"，庸医说这话的时候，你把树据为己有。）坐在小树林或者森林中，与这些默默无语的朋友为伴，回忆往事，陷入沉思。

追溯一棵树的根源得到的启示——也许从土地、岩石、动物身上获得的最伟大的道德启示同样是内在属性，无论旁观者（评论家）如何猜想或者评论，无论他喜欢抑或厌恶，都坚守自己的初衷。更糟糕的是——我们之间常常出现的流行疾病，我们的文学、教育、待人态度（甚至待己态度）之间常常出现的问题和疾病一样看起来不会造成困难，或者根本就没有困难，只是健全的、慢慢生长的、终年存在的人性本质，书籍、友情、婚姻的本质——人类无形的根基，紧紧地连接在一起？

---

1 affiliate /əˈfɪlieɪt/　　v.　隶属于
2 malady /ˈmælədi/　　n.　疾病
3 perennial /pəˈreniəl/　　adj.　终年的，持久的

含英咀华

在本文中，作者首先以诗人的眼睛，让读者看到一棵茂盛的黄白杨的雄伟身姿，然后又用诗人的语言去赞美这棵树的品质，最后用诗人的敏锐思考，告诉读者不要受外界的干扰，坚守自己的初衷。一棵树默默无闻地生存奉献，而人们却能从中获取丰富的人生哲理。

Philip Gulley

菲利普·格利

菲利普·格利（1973– ）美国教育专家，同时也是美国一些教育杂志的专栏作家，写了很多有关教育子女方面的文章。

Growing Roots

When I was growing up, I had an old neighbor named Dr. Gibbs. He didn't look like any doctor I'd ever known. He never yelled at us for playing in his yard. I remember him as someone who was a lot nicer than circumstances warranted[1].

When Dr. Gibbs wasn't saving lives, he was planting trees. His house sat on ten acres, and his life's goal was to make it a forest.

The good doctor had some interesting theories concerning plant husbandry[2]. He came from the "No pain, no gain" school of horticulture[3]. He never watered his new trees, which flew in the face of conventional wisdom. Once I asked why. He said that watering plants spoiled them, and that if you water them, each successive tree generation will grow weaker and weaker. So you have to make things rough for them and weed out the weenie[4] trees early on.

He talked about how watering trees made for shallow roots, and how trees that weren't watered had to grow deep roots in search of moisture. I took him to mean that deep roots were to be treasured.

1 warrant /ˈwɒrənt/ v. 使有（正当）理由，成为……的根据
2 husbandry /ˈhʌzbəndri/ n. 农牧业
3 horticulture /ˈhɔːtɪkʌltʃə(r)/ n. 园艺（学）
4 weenie /ˈwiːni/ adj. 细小的，微小的

成长的树根

在我还是小孩子的时候，我有一个老邻居叫吉布斯医生。他不像我所认识的任何一个医生。他从不因为我们在他庭院里玩耍就对我们大喊大叫。我记得他是一个非常和蔼的人。

吉布斯医生不拯救人生命的时候就去种树。他的住所占地10英亩，他的人生目标就是将它变成一片森林。

这个好医生对于如何耕种有一番有趣的理论。他来自一个"不劳无获"的园艺学校。他从不浇灌他新种的树，这显然与常理相悖。有一次我问他为什么。他说浇水会毁了这些树，如果浇水，每一代成活的树会变得越来越娇弱。所以你得把它们的生长环境变得艰苦些，尽早淘汰那些弱不禁风的树。

他还告诉我用水浇灌的树的根是如何的浅，而那些没有浇水的树的根必须钻入深深的泥土以获得水分。我将他的话理解为：深根是十分宝贵的。

So he never watered his trees. He'd plant an oak and, instead of watering it every morning, he'd beat it with a rolled-up newspaper. Smack! Slap! Pow! I asked him why he did that, and he said it was to get the tree's attention.

Dr. Gibbs went to glory[1] a couple of years after I left home. Every now and again, I walked by his house and looked at the trees that I'd watched him plant some twenty-five years ago. They're granite[2] strong now. Big and robust[3]. Those trees wake up in the morning and beat their chests and drink their coffee black[4].

I planted a couple of trees a few years back and carried water to them for a solid summer. I sprayed them. I prayed over them. The whole nine yards. Two years of coddling[5] has resulted in trees that expect to be waited on hand and foot. Whenever a cold wind blows in, they tremble and chatter their branches. Sissy trees.

Funny things about those trees of Dr. Gibbs'. Adversity and deprivation[6] seemed to benefit them in ways comfort and ease never could.

Every night before I go to bed, I check on my two sons. I stand over them and watch their little bodies, the rising and falling of life within. I often pray for them. Mostly I pray that their lives

所以他从不给他的树浇水。他种了一棵橡树，每天早上，他不是给它浇水，而是用一张卷起的报纸抽它。啪！噼！砰！我问他为什么这样做，他说是为了引起树的注意。

在我离家几年后，吉布斯医生就去世了。偶尔我经过他的房子，看着25年前我曾注视他种下的那些树。如今它们已是像石头一样结实了。枝繁叶茂、生气勃勃。这些树在早晨醒过来，拍打着胸脯，啜饮着苦难的汁水。

几年前我也种下了两三棵树。整整一个夏天我都坚持为它们浇水。为它们喷杀虫剂，为它们祈祷。整整9平方码大的地方。两年的悉心呵护，结果导致它们习惯了被无微不至地照顾。每当寒风吹起，它们就发抖，枝叶直打战。娇里娇气的两棵树。

吉布斯医生的树真是有趣。逆境和折磨带给它们的益处似乎是舒适和安逸永远无法给予的。

每天晚上睡觉前，我都要看看两个儿子。我俯视着他们那幼小的身体，生命就在其中起落沉浮。我总是为他们祈祷，总是祈祷他们的生活能一

---

1 go to glory 死
2 granite /ˈɡrænɪt/ n. 花岗石，坚如磐石
3 robust /rə(ʊ)ˈbʌst/ adj. 强健的，苗壮的
4 black (coffee) 此处喻指树所遭受的磨难
5 coddle /ˈkɒdl/ vt. 悉心照料
6 deprivation /ˌdeprɪˈveɪʃn/ n. 剥夺，丧失

will be easy. But lately I've been thinking that it's time to change my prayer.

This change has to do with the inevitability of cold winds that hit us at the core. I know my children are going to encounter hardship, and I'm praying they won't be naive. There's always a cold wind blowing somewhere.

So I'm changing my prayer. Because life is tough, whether we want it to be or not. Too many times we pray for ease, but that's a prayer seldom met. What we need to do is pray for roots that reach deep into the Eternal, so when the rains fall and the winds blow, we won't be swept asunder[1].

帆风顺。但后来我想是该改变我的祈祷词的时候了。

这改变与不可避免吹在我们要害的寒风有关。我知道我的孩子们将遇到困难，我祈祷他们不要太幼稚。在某些地方总会有寒风吹过。

所以我改变了我的祈祷词。因为不管我们愿不愿意，生活总是艰难的。我们已祈祷了太多的安逸，但却少有实现。我们所需要做的是祈祷深植我们的信念之根，这样我们就不会被雨打风吹所伤害。

一叶知秋　脚踏实地

---

1 **asunder** /əˈsʌndə(r)/　*adv.*　碎，散

含英咀华

本文作者以"成长的树根"来比喻"一个人的成长"可谓是立意新颖，见解独到，尤其是对天下所有的父母。每个父母每天对孩子的祈祷永远都是"幸福，快乐，一帆风顺"这样的词汇，但每个人的人生和成长经历都不会是一帆风顺的，成功的背后总是一条布满荆棘的道路。所以与其给孩子美好的祝福，不如让他们早早懂得生活的艰辛和成长中所遇到的困难。文章内容发人深省，值得读者品味。

Henry David Thoreau
亨利·大卫·梭罗

亨利·大卫·梭罗(1818~1862)，美国散文家、诗人、自然主义者、改革家和哲学家。梭罗的著作都是根据他在大自然中的体验写成。1839年他和哥哥在梅里马克河上划船漂游，写成《在康科德与梅里马克河上一周》(*A Week on the Concord and Merrimack Rivers, 1849*)，发表了他对自然、人生和文艺问题的见解。他的代表作《瓦尔登湖》(*Walden, 1854*)记录了他于1845年至1847年在康科德附近的瓦尔登湖畔度过的一段隐居生活。在他笔下，自然、人以及超验主义理想交融汇合，浑然一体。他是十九世纪超验主义运动的重要代表人物。他的文章简练有力，朴实自然，富有思想内容，在美国十九世纪散文中独树一帜。他的思想对英国工党、印度的甘地(*Mohandas Karamchand Gandhi, 1869~1948*)与美国黑人领袖马丁·路德·金(*Martin Luther King, Jr., 1929~1968*)等人都有很大的影响。

Love Your Life

However mean your life is, meet it and live it; do not shun it and call it hard names. It is not so bad as you are. It looks poorest when you are richest. The fault-finder[1] will find faults in paradise. Love your life, poor as it is. You may perhaps have some pleasant, thrilling, glorious hours, even in a poor-house. The setting sun is reflected from the windows of the almshouse[2] as brightly as from the rich man's abode[3]; the snow melts before its door as early in the spring. I do not see but a quiet mind may live as contentedly there, and have as cheering thoughts, as in a palace. The town's poor seem to me often to live the most independent lives of any. Maybe they are simply great enough to receive without misgiving[4]. Most think that they are above being supported by the town; but it often happens that they are not above supporting themselves by dishonest means, which should be more disreputable. Cultivate poverty like a garden herb[5], like sage. Do not trouble yourself much to get new things, whether clothes or friends. Turn the old, return to them. Things do not change;

1 fault-finder /'fɔːlt'faɪndə/   n.   吹毛求疵的人
2 almshouse /'ɑːmzhaʊs/   n.   济贫院
3 abode /ə'bəʊd/   n.   住处，住所
4 misgiving /ˌmɪs'gɪvɪŋ/   n.   疑虑
5 herb /hɜːb/   n.   药草，香草

热爱生活

不论你的生活如何卑贱，你都要勇敢地面对它，不要躲避它，更别用恶言咒骂它；生活不像你想得那么糟。你最富有的时候，倒是看似最穷。吹毛求疵的人就是在天堂里也能找到缺点。你要爱你的生活，无论它多么贫穷。即使在济贫院里，你也还有愉悦、振奋、辉煌的时候。夕阳照在济贫院的窗上所反射的光芒如同照在富户人家窗上所反射的光芒一样光彩夺目；到了早春的时候，门前的积雪同样会融化。我唯一能看到的是，一个心态平和的人，在哪里都会像在皇宫中一样，生活得心满意足而富有愉快的思想。在我看来，城镇中的穷人倒往往是过着最独立不羁的生活。或许他们的伟大之处就在于坦然地接受而不顾虑重重。大多数人对于城镇的恩惠不屑一顾；可是事实上不靠城镇来支援他们，他们则往往利用了不正当的手段来对付生活，他们是毫不超脱的，是不体面的。视贫穷

we change. Sell your clothes and keep your thoughts.

God will see that you do not want society. If I were confined[1] to a corner of a garret[2] all my days, like a spider, the world would be just as large to me while I had my thoughts about me. The philosopher said: "From an army of three divisions one can take away its general, and put it in disorder, from the man the most abject[3] and vulgar[4] one can not take away his thought." Do not seek so anxiously to be developed, to subject yourself to many influences to be played on, it is all dissipation[5]. Humility like darkness reveals the heavenly lights. The shadows of poverty and meanness gather around us, "and lo! Creation widens our view." We are often reminded that if there were bestowed[6] on us the wealth of Croesus[7], our aims must still be the same, and our means essentially the same. Moreover, if you are restricted in your range by poverty, if you can not buy books and newspapers, for instance, you are but confined to the most significant and vital experiences; you are compelled[8] to deal with the material which yields the most sugar and the most starch[9]. It is life near the bone where

1 confine /kən'faɪn/ v. 限制，闭居
2 garret /'ɡærət/ n. 阁楼，顶楼，头
3 abject /'æbdʒekt/ adj. 不幸的，可怜的，悲惨的
4 vulgar /'vʌlɡə(r)/ adj. 粗俗的
5 dissipation /ˌdɪsɪ'peɪʃn/ n. 浪费
6 bestow /bɪ'stəʊ/ v. 授予，适用
7 Croesus /'kriːsəs/ n. 克罗伊斯王，大富豪，大财主
8 compel /kəm'pel/ v. 强迫，迫使
9 starch /staːtʃ/ n. 淀粉

如园中之花而像圣人一样耕植它吧！不要费尽心机去寻找新花样了，不管是新朋友还是新衣服。让旧物常新，又回归旧物。万物不变，是我们在变。卖掉衣服，保留你的思想吧。

上帝会见证，你并不想融入社会。倘若我整天如同蜘蛛那样被局限于阁楼的一个角落，可我还有我的思想，那么世界还是原来那么大。曾有位哲人这么说："三军可夺帅也，匹夫不可夺志也。"不要迫切地谋求自己的发展，也不要让各种影响干扰自己，这一切都是浪费。因为谦卑就像黑暗一样，更凸显出天国之光。贫穷与卑贱的影子一直纠集在我们左右："看啊！天地万物开阔了我们的视野。"我们常常得到警示，如果上帝赋予我们和克罗伊斯王一样的财富，我们的目标一定不会改变，我们的方式也不会改变。此外，如果贫困束缚了你，比如说你没钱买书和报纸，你的经验只是局限于最有意义、最为重要的那一部分；你被迫和那些糖和淀粉含量最高的物质打交道。越接近生命的本质才最能品味出它甜美的地方。你不可能成为一个不务正业的人。宽

105

it is sweetest. You are defended from being a trifler[1]. No man loses ever on a lower level by magnanimity[2] on a higher. Superfluous wealth can buy superfluities[3] only. Money is not required to buy one necessary of the soul.

宏大量，不会让曾在较低层次的人在较高层次失去什么。过多财富只能买到多余的物品。而人所必需的灵魂是用金钱买不到的。

---

1 **trifler** /'traɪflə/   *n.*   不务正业的人；吊儿郎当的人
2 **magnanimity** /ˌmæɡnəˈnɪməti/   *n.*   宽大宏量，度量大
3 **superfluity** /ˌsuːpəˈfluːəti/   *n.*   多余，过剩

含英咀华

　　本文短小而有力度，作者使用了矛盾修辞法说明快乐与否和物质财富的多少并不成正比；你最富有时反而最贫困，穷人的生活也许最快乐。所以，不要在乎财富，"过多财富只能买到过多的物品。而人所必需的灵魂是用金钱买不到的。"那么，就让我们热爱生活，即使做一个物质上的穷人，我们也依然会为自己是精神上的富人而快乐。

Jack Canfield

杰克·坎菲尔德

杰克·坎菲尔德（1944~），美国心理学专家、专栏作家和社会工作者。

Follow Your Dream

追随梦想

I have a friend named Monty Roberts who owns a horse ranch in San Ysidro. He has let me use his house to put on fund-raising events to raise money for youth at risk programs.

The last time I was there he introduced me by saying, "I want to tell you why I let Jack use my house. It all goes back to[1] a story about a young man who was the son of an itinerant[2] horse trainer who would go from stable to stable, race track[3] to race track, farm to farm and ranch to ranch, training horses. As a result, the boy's high school career was continually interrupted. When he was a senior, he was asked to write a paper about what he wanted to be and do when he grew up.

"That night he wrote a seven-page paper describing his goal of someday owning a horse ranch[4]. He wrote about his dream in great detail and he even drew a diagram of a 200-acre ranch, showing the location of all the buildings, the stables and the track. Then he drew a detailed floor plan for a 4,000-square-foot house that would sit on a 200-acre dream ranch.

我有个朋友叫蒙提·罗伯兹，他在圣伊西德罗有个牧马场。我常借用他的住宅举办募款活动，以便为帮助青少年的风险计划筹备基金。

上次活动时，他在致辞中讲道："我让杰克借用住宅是有原因的。这故事跟一个小男孩有关，他的父亲是位巡回马术师，他从小就必须跟着父亲东奔西走，训练马匹。男孩的求学过程并不顺利。初中时，有次老师叫全班同学写报告，题目是长大后的志愿。"

"那晚他洋洋洒洒写了七张纸，描述他的伟大志愿，那就是想拥有一座属于自己的赛马场，并且仔细画了一张200亩农场的设计图，上面标有马厩、跑道等的位置。然后还在这200英亩梦幻农场上画了一栋占地4000平方英尺的豪宅设计图。"

---

1 go back to 追溯到。例如：Let's go back to what the chairman said earlier. （让我们回到主席先前说的问题上。）
2 itinerant /aɪˈtɪnərənt/ *adj.* 巡回的
3 race track 赛马场
4 ranch /rɑːntʃ/ *n.* 牧场

"He put a great deal of his heart into the project and the next day he handed it in to his teacher. Two days later he received his paper back. On the front page was a large red F with a note that read, 'See me after class.'

"The boy with the dream went to see the teacher after class and asked, 'Why did I receive an F?'

"The teacher said, 'This is an unrealistic dream for a young boy like you. You have no money. You come from an itinerant family. You have no resources. Owning a horse ranch requires a lot of money. You have to buy the land. You have to pay for the original breeding stock and later you'll have to pay large stud[1] fees. There's no way you could ever do it.' Then the teacher added, 'If you will rewrite this paper with a more realistic goal, I will reconsider your grade.'"

"The boy went home and thought about it long and hard. He asked his father what he should do. His father said, 'Look, son, you have to make up your own mind on this. However, I think it is a very important decision for you.'"

"Finally, after sitting with it for a week, the boy turned in the same paper, making no changes at all. He stated, 'You can keep the F and I'll keep my dream.'"

Monty then turned to the assembled group and said, "I tell you this story because you are

"他花了好大心血把报告完成，第二天交给了老师。两天后他拿回了报告，第一页上打了一个又红又大的F，旁边还写了一行字：下课后来见我。"

"脑中充满幻想的他下课后带着报告去找老师：'为什么给我不及格？'"

"老师回答道：'对于你这样的男孩来说，这是一个不切实际的梦想。你没钱，居无定所，什么都没有。建赛马场是需要很多钱的；你要买地、买纯种马匹、以后还要付种马费。你别太好高骛远了。'他接着又说，'如果你肯重写一个比较不离谱的志愿，我会重新给你打分。'"

"这男孩回家后反复思量，然后征询父亲的意见。父亲只是告诉他：'儿子，你必须自己拿主意，我认为对你来说这是个非常重要的决定。'"

"再三考虑好几天后，他决定原稿交回，一个字都没改。他告诉老师：'你可以给我不及格，但我不会放弃梦想。'"

蒙提此时向众人表示："我提起这故事，是因为各位

---

1 **stud** /stʌd/ *n.* 种马

sitting in my 4,000-square-foot house in the middle of my 200-acre horse ranch. I still have that school paper framed over the fireplace." He added, "The best part of the story is that two summers ago that same schoolteacher brought 30 kids to camp out on my ranch for a week." When the teacher was leaving, he said, 'Look, Monty, I can tell you this now. When I was your teacher, I was something of a dream stealer. During those years I stole a lot of kids' dreams. Fortunately you had enough gumption[1] not to give up on yours.'"

Don't let anyone steal your dreams. Follow your heart, no matter what.

现在就坐在200亩农场中央占地4000平方英尺的房子里。那份初中时写的报告现在还挂在壁炉上面的镜框里。"他顿了一下又说："有意思的是，两年前的夏天，那位老师带了30个学生来我的农场露营一星期。离开之前，他对我说：'蒙提，说来有些惭愧。作为你的老师，我曾泼过你冷水。这些年来，我打击过不少学生的梦想。幸亏你进取心不减，坚持了下来。'"

不要让任何人摧毁了你的梦想。无论在什么情况下，都要坚定信念。

---

1 gumption /ˈɡʌmpʃn/   n.   进取精神，勇气

含英咀华

在本文中，作者通过一个小故事来告诉读者梦想的力量。这个世界如此突飞猛进地变化和发展，跟人类的梦想是无法分割的。我们要尊重有梦想的人，无论他的梦想是多么荒诞或者遥不可及。活着必须是要有梦想的，无论是高尚还是简单，无论是远大还是卑微。正因为有着梦想或者理想才会把你和动物的浑浑噩噩区别开来。坚持自己的梦想，给自己的梦想插上翅膀，在追寻那些梦想的过程中，你才能体会到所有的欢乐和痛苦，你才能明白生命不过是一场寻找并且不断修正梦想的旅程，你才会对那些和你一样有着梦想的人惺惺相惜。在读完上面的文章后，也许你就会明白梦想的真正含义。文章语言平实，通俗，但发人深省。句子结构简单，拉近了作者和读者之间的距离。

Benjamin Franklin
本杰明·富兰克林

本杰明·富兰克林(1706~1790)，美国著名的政治家与科学家。他是美国革命时期重要的领导人之一，参与了多项重要文件的草拟，并曾出任美国驻法国大使，成功取得法国支持美国独立。他还曾经进行多项关于电的实验，并且发明了避雷针。他一生最真实的写照是他自己所说过的一句话："诚实和勤勉，应该成为你永久的伴侣。"

The Whistle

I received my dear friend's two letters, one for Wednesday and one for Saturday. This is again Wednesday. I do not deserve one for today, because I have not answered the former. But, indolent[1] as I am, and averse[2] to writing, the fear of having no more of your pleasing epistles[3], if I do not contribute to the correspondence[4], obliges me to take up my pen; and as Mr. B. has kindly sent me word that he sets out tomorrow to see you, instead of spending this Wednesday evening, as I have done its namesakes, in your delightful company, I sit down to spend it in thinking of you, in writing to you, and in reading over and over again your letters.

I am charmed with your description of Paradise[5], and with your plan of living there; and I approve much of your conclusion, that, in the meantime, we should draw all the good we can from this world. In my opinion we might all draw more good from it than we do, and suffer less evil, if we would take care not to give too much for whistles. For to me it seems that most of the unhappy people we meet with are become so by

1 indolent /ˈɪndələnt/　*adj.*　懒惰的
2 averse /əˈvɜːs/　*adj.*　厌恶的，反对的
3 epistle /ɪˈpɪsl/　*n.*　书信
4 correspondence /ˌkɒrəˈspɒndəns/　*n.*　来往信件；通信
5 Paradise /ˈpærədaɪs/　*n.*　天堂

哨子

　　亲爱的朋友，我已经收到你两封来信了，周三和周六各一封。一眨眼，又到周三了。我不再期许今天再收到你的来信了，因为之前的信我还没来得及回呢。我承认自己懒惰，也不喜欢写信，可是我又害怕自己不回信就会再也收不到你那令人愉悦的来信。想到这，我不得不拿起笔来。B先生好心地告诉我，他打算明天去拜访你，而不是在今天晚上。坐在桌前，心里想着有你快乐的相伴，我整个晚上都在想念你，在给你写回信，还一遍又一遍地阅读你的来信。

　　我沉醉于你所描述的天堂，羡慕你去那里生活的计划，并认同你大多数的观点，与此同时，我们可以一起构想这个世界上一切美好的事物。在我看来，如果我们注意不在哨子上付出太多的话，我们就可以获得比我们现在拥有的更美好的事物，也会少遭受一些痛苦。因为对我来说，大部分闷闷不乐的人都是由于对这一

neglec of that caution.

You ask what I mean? You love stories, and will excuse my telling one of myself.

When I was a child of seven years old, my friends, on a holiday, filled my pocket with coppers. I went directly to a shop where they sold toys for children; and being charmed with the sound of a whistle, that I met by the way in the hands of another boy, I voluntarily[1] offered and gave all my money for one. I then came home, and went whistling all over the house, much pleased with my whistle, but disturbing all the family. My brothers, and sisters, and cousins, understanding the bargain I had made, told me I had given four times as much for it as it was worth; put me in mind what good things I might have bought with the rest of the money; and laughed at me so much for my folly[2], that I cried with vexation[3]; and the reflection gave me more chagrin[4] than the whistle gave me pleasure.

This, however, was afterwards of use to me, the impression continuing on my mind; so that often, when I was tempted[5] to buy some unnecessary things, I said to myself, "Don't give too much for the whistle; and I saved my money."

As I grew up, came into the world, and observed the actions of men, I thought I met with

---

1　voluntarily /ˈvɒləntrəli/　adv.　自动地；无偿的
2　folly /ˈfɒli/　n.　愚蠢，荒唐事，轻松歌舞剧
3　vexation /vekˈseɪʃn/　n.　恼怒
4　chagrin /ˈʃæɡrɪn/　n.　懊恼
5　tempt /tempt/　v.　诱惑；引起；冒……之险

警示不予理睬而遭遇不幸。

你可能会问，我说的是什么意思。你喜欢听故事，那就请允许我讲一个发生在我身上的故事吧。

我七岁的时候，有一次过节，朋友们给我的衣袋里塞满了铜币。我立刻向一家卖儿童玩具的店铺跑去。半路上，我却被另一个男孩手中哨子的叫声吸引住了，于是用我所有的铜币换了他这个哨子。回到家里，我非常得意，吹着哨子满屋子转，却打扰了家人。我的哥哥、姐姐和表亲们知道我这个交易后便告诉我，为这个哨子我付出了相当于原价四倍的钱。他们还使我懂得，用那些多付的钱可以买到多少好东西啊。大伙儿都笑话我傻，竟使我懊恼得哭了。回想起来那只哨子给我带来的悔恨远远超过了给我的快乐。

不过，这件事情后来却对我很有用处，它一直保留在我的记忆中。因此，当我打算买一些不必要的东西时，我便常常对自己说，不要为哨子花费太多，于是我就把钱省下了。

我长大了走进社会，观察人们的作为，感到我遇到的很多很多的人，他们都为一个哨子付出了过高的代价。

many, very many, who gave too much for the whistle.

When I saw one too ambitious of court favor[1], sacrificing his time in attendance on levees[2], his repose[3], his liberty, his virtue, and perhaps his friends, to attain[4] it, I have said to myself, "This man gives too much for his whistle."

When I saw another fond of popularity, constantly employing himself in political bustles[5], neglecting his own affairs, and ruining them by that neglect. "He pays, indeed," said I, "too much for his whistle."

If I knew a miser[6], who gave up every kind of comfortable living, all the pleasure of doing good to others, all the esteem[7] of his fellow-citizens, and the joys of benevolent[8] friendship, for the sake of accumulating wealth. "Poor man," said I, "you pay too much for your whistle."

When I met with a man of pleasure, sacrificing every laudable[9] improvement of the mind, or of his fortune, to mere corporeal sensations, and ruining his health in their pursuit. "Mistaken man," said I, "you are providing pain for yourself, instead of pleasure; you give too much for your whistle."

1 court favor　求宠（于人），拍（人）马屁
2 levee /'levi/　n.　专为某人举行的招待会
3 repose /rɪ'pəʊz/　n.　休息，睡眠，静止
4 attain /ə'teɪn/　v.　达到，获得
5 bustle /'bʌsl/　n.　忙乱嘈杂
6 miser /'maɪzə/　n.　守财奴，吝啬鬼
7 esteem /ɪ'stiːm/　n.　尊敬
8 benevolent /bɪ'nevələnt/　adj.　仁慈的，乐善好施的
9 laudable /'lɔːdəbl/　adj.　值得称赞的

当我看见一个人过分热衷于趋炎附势，为寻求会见而不惜牺牲自己的睡眠、自由、品德甚至朋友时，我便对自己说，这个人为了他的哨子付出了过高的代价。

当我看到另一个人醉心于名望，无休止地投身于政界的纷扰之中，却忽视了自己的事，最后因为这种忽视而毁了自己的人生时，我说，他的确也为了他的哨子付出了过高的代价。

如果我得知一个守财奴为了积累财产，宁愿放弃各种舒适的生活，为别人做好事的一切乐趣，所有的同乡们对他的尊重，以及由慷慨无私的友谊带来的快乐时，我说，可怜的人啊，为了你的哨子，你付出了过高的代价。

当我遇到一个寻欢作乐的人，他仅仅为了追求肉体上的享受，牺牲一切精神或物质上值得称道的改进，甚至不惜损坏了自己的身体时，我说，误入歧途的人啊，你真是有福不享自找苦吃；为了你的哨子，你付出了太高的代价啊。

当我看到一个人沉迷于外表，迷恋漂亮的装束，讲究的住宅，上等的家具，精致的

If I see one fond of appearance, or fine clothes, fine houses, fine furniture, fine equipages[1], all above his fortune, for which he contracts debts, and ends his career in a prison. "Alas!" say I, "he has paid dear, very dear, for his whistle."

When I see a beautiful sweet-tempered girl married to an ill-natured brute of a husband. "What a pity," say I, "that she should pay so much for a whistle!"

In short, I conceive that great part of the miseries of mankind are brought upon them by the false estimates they have made of the value of things, and by their giving too much for their whistles.

Yet I ought to have charity for these unhappy people, when I consider that, with all this wisdom of which I am boasting, there are certain things in the world so tempting, for example, the apples of King John, which happily are not to be bought; for if they were put to sale by auction, I might very easily be led to ruin myself in the purchase, and find that I had once more given too much for the whistle.

Adieu[2], my dear friend, and believe me ever yours very sincerely and with unalterable[3] affection.

设备，为得到这一切，他人不敷出，债台高筑，最后被投进监狱时，我说，天啊!为了他的哨子，他付出了太高太高的代价。

当我看到一个美丽动人、性情温顺的姑娘嫁给一个生性恶劣、人面兽心的丈夫时，我说，多么遗憾呀，她为了一只哨子付出了太高的代价。

总之，我认为，人们所遭受的大部分不幸，都是由于他们对事物的价值做出错误的估价而造成的，都为他们的哨子付出了太高的代价。

但是我应当对这些不幸的人们抱以同情，我想到，尽管我为具有所有这些智慧而骄傲，但在这个世界上，有些东西确实是那样地诱惑人，比如，约翰王的苹果，幸好那不是能买到的。如果一旦这些苹果被拍卖，我很可能会轻易地在这交易中将自己毁灭，然后发现自己又一次为了那个哨子付出了过高的代价。

再见，我亲爱的朋友。请相信我永远是你真诚的朋友，我对你的情谊永远不会改变。

1 equipage /ˈekwəpɪdʒ/ n. 装备，设备
2 adieu /əˈdjuː/ int. 再见，再会
3 unalterable /ʌnˈɔːltərəbl/ adj. 不能改变的

116

含英咀华

　　本文是富兰克林一篇有名的散文，文中把权利、功名、利禄、财富、爱情都比作他童年时用"昂贵代价"换来的哨子，它们时时发出奇异玄奥的哨音，诱惑着每一个人。值得我们回味的是在我们现实生活中，为"微不足道的哨子"而付出高昂代价的人和事，屡见不鲜。人的一生，不管愿不愿意，总会遇上这样那样的"哨子"，不妨把它们看淡些，时时保持一份平淡的心绪，时时想到生活里还有更加珍贵的东西，这样，也许可以少付一点代价。

他山之石
可以攻玉

Robert Louis Stevenson
罗伯特·路易斯·史蒂文森

罗伯特·路易斯·史蒂文森(1850~1894)，英国新浪漫主义小说家兼小品文作家，生于爱丁堡，毕业于爱丁堡大学法律系，但他最大的兴趣在文学方面。1878年，史蒂文森出版了他的第一本游记《内河航程》(An Inland Voyage)。一年后，又出版了《骑驴漫游记》(Travels with a Donkey in the Cévennes)。从此，他放弃律师业务，潜心写作，在短短的一生中写下了大量的散文、游记、随笔、小说和诗歌。主要作品有小说《金银岛》(Treasure Island, 1883)、《化身博士》(Strange Case of Dr Jekyll and Mr Hyde, 1886)、《绑架》(Kidnapped, 1886)等。他的作品情节奇妙浪漫，文笔优美雅致。

El Dorado

黄金国

It seems as if a great deal were attainable in a world where there are so many marriages and decisive battles, and where we all, at certain hours of the day, and with great gusto[1] and dispatch[2], stow a portion of victuals finally and irretrievably[3] into the bag which contains us. And it would seem also, on a hasty view, that the attainment of as much as possible was the one goal of man's contentious[4] life. And yet, as regards the spirit, this is but a semblance. We live in an ascending scale when we live happily, one thing leading to another in an endless series. There is always a new horizon for onward-looking men, and although we dwell on a small planet, immersed in petty business and not enduring beyond a brief period of years[5], we are so constituted that our hopes are inaccessible, like stars, and the term of hoping is prolonged until the term of life. To be truly happy is a question of how we begin and not of how we end, of what we want and not of what we have. An aspiration[6] is a joy for ever, a possession as solid as a landed estate, a fortune

人生在世，能够得到的东西似乎很多。世间充满联姻婚嫁和决战厮杀。无论身在何处，在每天的固定时刻，我们最终都会不可避免地将一份食物津津有味且迅速地吞入腹中。乍一看，似乎竭尽全力去获取是一个人喧嚣人生的一个目标。但是，从精神层面上来看，这只不过是一个假象。当我们生活得很幸福时，我们身处在一个上升的阶段，好事连连，永无止境。目光长远的人的视野总是开阔的；尽管我们居住在一个个小星球上，为日常琐事而忙，生命短暂，但我们认为希望就像群星那样遥不可及，生命不息，希望不止。真正的幸福在于我们怎样开始而不是怎样结束，在于我们想要什么而不是我们拥有什么。渴望永远是一种快乐，是像不动产一样坚实的财产，是我们用之不竭、年年给予我们快乐的财富。要想拥有这一切就要达到精神上的富有。除非我们有兴趣，否则生活就是一部平

1 gusto /ˈɡʌstəu/ *n.* 热情，兴致，精力
2 dispatch /dɪˈspætʃ/ *v.* 派遣 （with dispatch 迅速而有效）
3 irretrievably /ˌɪrɪˈtriːvəbli/ *adv.* 不可挽回地
4 contentious /kənˈtenʃəs/ *adj.* 好争吵的，爱争论的
5 immersed in ... a brief period of years 是非谓语动词形式，修饰 although we dwell on a small planet
6 aspiration /ˌæspəˈreɪʃn/ *n.* 热望，渴望

which we can never exhaust and which gives us year by year a revenue of pleasurable activity. To have many of these is to be spiritually rich. Life is only a very dull and ill-directed theatre unless we have some interests in the piece; and to those who have neither art nor science, the world is a mere arrangement of colors, or a rough footway where they may very well break their shins. It is in virtue of his own desires and curiosities that any man continues to exist with even patience, that he is charmed by the look of things and people, and that he wakens every morning with a renewed appetite[1] for work and pleasure. Desire and curiosity are the two eyes through which he sees the world in the most enchanted colors: it is they that make women beautiful or fossils interesting: and the man may squander[2] his estate and come to beggary, but if he keeps these two amulets[3] he is still rich in the possibilities of pleasure. Suppose he could take one meal so compact and comprehensive that he should never hunger any more; suppose him, at a glance, to take in all the features of the world and allay the desire for knowledge; suppose him to do the like in any province of experience — would not that man be in a poor way for amusement ever after?

One who goes touring on foot with a single

淡枯燥的戏剧。对于那些既没有艺术天赋也没有科学灵感的人来说，世界只不过是颜色的混合体，或是一条崎岖的小路，走在其上他们很可能会摔伤小腿。正是人类的渴望和好奇心才使得我们充满耐心地继续生存；才使得我们被芸芸众生而吸引；才使得我们每日清晨醒来都会以新的面貌愉快地投入到工作中。渴望和好奇是人们用来观察这个五彩缤纷的世界的两只眼睛，它们使女性美丽、化石有趣，只要有这两道护身符，即使他将财产挥霍而尽，沦为乞丐，他仍旧是快乐的。假设一个人吃了一顿紧凑而丰盛的饭菜，他将不会再挨饿；假设他一眼就把世间万象看透，那他对知识就不会那么渴求；假设他在每个生活的方方面面都是如此，那他从此以后还有什么乐趣可言么？

一位徒步旅行的人包中只装有一本书，他仔细研读，时常停下来思考，且经常掩卷沉思，凝望风景或观赏客栈里的字画。因为他害怕乐趣一旦没有了，剩下的旅途中他将孤寂

---

1 appetite /'æpɪtaɪt/　n.　爱好，欲望
2 squander /'skwɒndə(r)/　v.　浪费，使……散开
3 amulet /'æmjʊlət/　n.　护身符

volume in his knapsack reads with circumspection, pausing often to reflect, and often laying the book down to contemplate[1] the landscape or the prints in the inn parlor; for he fears to come to an end of his entertainment, and be left companionless on the last stages of his journey. A young fellow recently finished the works of Thomas Carlyle, winding up, if I remember aright, with the ten note-books upon Frederick the Great. "What!" cried the young fellow, in consternation[2], "is there no more Carlyle? Am I left to the daily papers?" A more celebrated instance is that of Alexander, who wept bitterly because he had no more worlds to subdue. And when Gibbon had finished the *Decline and Fall*, he had only a few moments of joy; and it was with a "sober melancholy" that he parted from his labors.

Happily we all shoot at the moon with ineffectual arrows; our hopes are set on inaccessible El Dorado; we come to an end of nothing here below. Interests are only plucked up to sow themselves again, like mustard[3]. You would think, when the child was born, there would be an end to trouble; and yet it is only the beginning of fresh anxieties; and when you have seen it through its teething and its education, and at last its marriage, alas! It is only to have new fears, new quivering sensibilities, with every day; and the health of

无伴。最近，一位年轻人读完了托马斯·卡莱尔的作品，如果我没记错的话，他整整做了十本关于腓特烈大帝的笔记。"什么？"这个年轻人惊叫到，"再也没有卡莱尔的作品了？我只好读报纸了吗？"一个更有名的例子是关于亚历山大的。他痛哭流涕，因为已没有国家让他去征服了。当吉本写完《罗马帝国兴亡史》后，只兴奋了一阵子，他怀着一种清醒而又忧郁的心情与他的劳动成果作别。

我们兴奋地把箭射向月亮，但都一无所获；我们的希望都寄托在遥不可及的黄金国上，我们无果而终。就像芥菜一样，收获兴趣只是为了下次的播种。孩子出生后你会认为，一切麻烦都会到此为止，其实这只是新的烦恼的开始。因为你要看着他成长，入学，最终成家，哎！每天都会有新的恐惧，新的复杂情感。子孙们的健康就像你的健康一样使你牵肠挂肚。同样，当你娶妻后，你会认为你已到了顶峰，可以步履舒缓地下坡了。

1 contemplate /'kɒntəmpleɪt/   v.   注视，沉思
2 consternation /ˌkɒnstə'neɪʃn/   n.   惊愕，恐怖
3 mustard /'mʌstəd/   n.   芥菜

your children's children grows as touching a concern as that of your own. Again, when you have married your wife, you would think you were got upon a hilltop, and might begin to go downward by an easy slope. But you have only ended courting to begin marriage. Falling in love and winning love are often difficult tasks to overbearing and rebellious spirits; but to keep in love is also a business of some importance, to which both man and wife must bring kindness and goodwill. The true love story commences at the altar, when there lies before the married pair a most beautiful contest of wisdom and generosity, and a life-long struggle towards an unattainable ideal. Unattainable? Ay, surely unattainable, from the very fact that they are two instead of one.

"Of making books there is no end," complained the Preacher; and did not perceive how highly he was praising letters as an occupation. There is no end, indeed, to make books or experiments, or to travel, or to gather wealth. Problem gives rise to problem. We may study for ever, and we are never as learned as we would. We have never made a statue worthy of our dreams. And when we have discovered a continent, or crossed a chain of mountains, it is only to find another ocean or another plain upon the further side. In the infinite universe there is room for our swiftest diligence and to spare. It is not like the works of Carlyle, which can be read to an end. Even in a corner of it, in a private park, or in the neighborhood

但这只是恋爱的结束，婚姻的开始。对于傲慢自大和桀骜不驯的人来说相爱和赢得爱情都是困难的；但维持爱情也很重要，要想做到这一点，夫妻之间必须相敬如宾。真正的爱情故事从圣坛开始，摆在每对新人面前的是一场关于智慧和大度的最壮观的竞争，且他们要为不可能实现的理想奋斗终生。不可能实现？啊，当然不可能实现了，这是因为他们是两个人而不是一个人。

布道者抱怨道，"著书无终"，但却没有觉察到他对作家这一行业的评价是多么的高。确实，著书立说、体验、旅行、积聚财富都是没有止境的。一个问题会引发另一个问题。我们必须终生学习，我们永远也不会如期望的那样博学。我们从来没有塑造出我们梦中的塑像。当我们发现一个新大陆或穿越一座山脉时，却发现在远方还有海洋和山川。宇宙茫茫，即使我们再勤勉也没有尽头。它不像卡莱尔的著作那样可以读完。即使一隅之地，在一个私人花园，在一个村庄附近，天气和季节的变化是这样的迅速无常，以致尽管我们终生生活其中，也总会对

of a single hamlet, the weather and the seasons keep so deftly[1] changing that although we walk there for a lifetime there will be always something new to startle[2] and delight us.

There is only one wish realizable on the earth; only one thing that can be perfectly attained: Death. And from a variety of circumstances we have no one to tell us whether it be worth attaining.

A strange picture we make on our way to our chimaeras[3], ceaselessly marching, grudging ourselves the time for rest; indefatigable[4], adventurous pioneers. It is true that we shall never reach the goal; it is even more than probable that there is no such place; and if we lived for centuries and were endowed with the powers of a god, we should find ourselves not much nearer what we wanted at the end. O toiling hands of mortals! O unwearied feet, traveling ye know not whither! Soon, soon, it seems to you, you must come forth on some conspicuous hilltop, and but a little way further, against the setting sun, descry[5] the spires of El Dorado. Little do ye know your own blessedness; for to travel hopefully is a better thing than to arrive, and the true success is to labor.

周围的新奇事物感到欣喜与惊讶。

世上只有一种可以实现的愿望；只有一样事物绝对能够得到：是死亡。死有百态，但无一人能告诉我们死究竟值不值得。

当我们不作休息，不停地走向幻想时，一幅奇异的画面展现出来：不知疲倦，勇于冒险的先锋。确实，我们永远不会到达目的地；甚至很可能不存在这样的地方；即使我们活上几百年，被赋予神的力量，最终也会发现自己并没有更接近所欲到达的目标。啊，辛劳的双手！啊，不知疲倦的双脚，并不知道向何方而去。就快要到了，你会觉得自己一定会登上某个光辉的山顶，但再走几步，在夕阳下，你就会看到黄金国那些尖尖的塔顶。你并不知道自己有多么幸福；因为满怀希望地前进，更胜于到达目的地。真正的成功就是奋斗。

1 deftly /'deftli/   adv.   灵巧地，敏捷地
2 startle /'stɑːtl/   v.   使惊讶
3 chimaera /kaɪ'mɪərə/   n.   幻想
4 indefatigable /ˌɪndɪ'fætɪɡəbl/   adj.   不知疲倦的
5 descry /dɪ'skraɪ/   v.   看出，看见，察看

含英咀华

　　本篇标题为西班牙文，意为"黄金国"，指人类理想中的乐园，揭示出只有通过不断的努力，才能挖掘幸福人生，只有为了理想坚持奋斗才能获得成功。文章开始，作者就点明题意：真正的幸福在于渴望，在于奋斗，而不是知足常乐。然后作者举出大量的实例来说明没有奋斗目标就会失去人生的快乐，最后作者告诉读者真正的成功就是奋斗的过程。

William Somerset Maugham

威廉·萨然塞特·毛姆

威廉·萨然塞特·毛姆(1874~1965)，英国小说家，在长篇小说、短篇小说和戏剧领域里都有所建树，先后出版了《人性的枷锁》(*Of Human Bondage, 1915*)、《兰贝斯的丽莎》(*Liza of Lambeth, 1897*)等畅销书。他的作品不仅有法国文学的浪漫和自然，还有英国文学的谨慎和机智。

On Motes and Beams

It is curious that our own offenses should seem so much less heinous[1] than the offenses of others. I suppose the reason is that we know all the circumstances that have occasioned[2] them and so manage to excuse in ourselves what we cannot excuse in others. We turn our attention away from our own defects, and when we are forced by untoward events to consider them, find it easy to condone[3] them. For all I know we are right to do this; they are part of us and we must accept the good and bad in ourselves together.

But when we come to judge others, it is not by ourselves as we really are that we judge them, but by an image that we have formed of ourselves from which we have left out everything that offends our vanity or would discredit us in the eyes of the world. To take a trivial instance: how scornful[4] we are when we catch someone out telling a lie; but who can say that he has never told one, but a hundred?

There is not much to choose between men. They are all a hotchpotch[5] of greatness

---

1 heinous /'heɪnəs/ adj. 可憎的，十恶不赦的
2 occasion /ə'keɪʒn/ v. 致使，惹起，引起
3 condone /kən'dəʊn/ v. 宽恕，原谅
4 scornful /'skɔːnfl/ adj. 轻蔑的
5 hotchpotch /'hɒtʃpɒtʃ/ n. 大杂烩

微尘与栋梁

让人奇怪的是，和别人的过错比起来，我们自身的过错往往不是那样的可恶。我想，其原因应该是我们知晓一切导致自己犯错的情况，因此能够设法谅解自己的错误，而别人的错误却不能谅解。我们对自己的缺点不甚关注，即便是深陷困境而不得不正视它们的时候，我们也会很容易宽恕自己。据我所知，我们这样做是正确的。缺点是我们自身的一部分，我们必须接纳自己的好和坏。

但是当我们评判别人的时候，情况就不同了。我们不是通过真实的自我来评判别人，而是用一种自我形象来评判，这种自我形象完全摒弃了在任何世人眼中会伤害到自己的虚荣或者体面的东西。举一个小例子来说：当觉察到别人说谎时，我们是多么蔑视他啊！但是，谁能够说自己从未说过谎？可能还不止一百次呢。

人和人之间没什么大的差别。他们皆是伟大与渺小，善良与邪恶，高尚与低俗的混合

and littleness, of virtue and vice, of nobility and baseness. Some have more strength of character, or more opportunity, and so in one direction or another give their instincts freer play, but potentially they are the same. For my part, I do not think I am any better or any worse than most people, but I know that if I set down every action in my life and every thought that has crossed my mind, the world would consider me as a monster of depravity[1]. The knowledge that these reveries are common to all men should inspire one with tolerance to oneself as well as to others. It is well also if they enable us to look upon our fellows, even the most eminent[2] and respectable, with humor, and if they lead us to take ourselves not too seriously.

体。有的人性格比较坚毅，机会也比较多，因而在这个或那个方面，能够更自由地发挥自己的禀赋，但是人类的潜能却都是相同的。至于我自己，我认为自己并不比大多数人更好或者更差，但是我知道，假如我记下我生命中的每一个举动和每一个掠过我脑海的想法的话，世界就会将我视为一个邪恶的怪物。每个人都会有这样的怪念头，这样的认识应当能够启发我们宽容自己，也宽容他人。同样，假如因此我们得以用幽默的态度看待他人，即使是天下最优秀最令人尊敬的人，而且假如我们也因此不把自己看得过于重要，那是很有裨益的。

---

1 depravity /dɪ'prævəti/ n. 堕落，腐败，邪恶
2 eminent /'emɪnənt/ adj. 著名的，卓越的

含英咀华

本文的"微尘与栋梁"指他人的小缺点与自己的大缺点，以此为篇名寓意深远，希冀借此申明责己与责人之道。文章庄谐雅致，清新如风，用机智幽默的语言启发大家对人不要过于苛刻，不要总是放大别人的缺点，却忽视自己的不足，人与人在本质上是没有区别的，所以我们要宽以待人。

Daniel N. Brown

丹尼尔·布朗

在英美一些发达国家，人们渐渐丧失了对生活的热情，在富足的生活中迷失方向，为了解决这一问题，一些有识之士开辟了一些网站并撰写文章来鼓舞大家过一种有意义、充满激情的生活，本文的作者就是其中一位。丹尼尔·布朗是圣经成功原则 *(biblical success principles)* 的倡导者和教师。他每周免费出版教导人们如何拥有"基督教徒成功秘密" *(Christian Prosperity Secrets)*。

The Power of Thoughts

How often have you gotten started on something new with great positive energy and everything went well in the beginning? Whether it was a new job, a new relationship, moving to a new area, a new project, anything. You started off with zeal[1] and passion. But after a while you grew tired. Your positive energy began to turn negative and your thoughts began to work against[2] you. Before you knew it you started creating things you didn't want.

It all started when you lost focus on what you wanted. Instead of creating what you wanted you started saying things like, I hate my job, my boyfriend/girlfriend is difficult, I don't like it here anymore, and the pattern continued. Then things get progressively worse and you wonder what went wrong.

I believe this is what went wrong. You lost control over your thoughts and stopped creating the things you wanted in your life.

Thoughts are powerful forces of energy and can only come from your own mind. Since you are the only person in charge of your mind, you create the thoughts that create the circumstances

1 zeal /ziːl/　n.　热情
2 work against　对……不利　例如：I had to cycle all the way to work against the wind.（我不得不一路顶着风去上班。）

思想的力量

你是否常常以非常积极的精力开始新事物，而且在开始的时候一切顺利？无论是开始一项新的工作，建立一种新的关系，还是迈向一个新的领域，开展一个新的项目等等。开始时你充满热情和激情。但过了一阵子，你感到累了。你积极的能量开始转为消极的，你的思想开始和你作对。你还没来得及了解状况，你不想要的东西就出现了。

当你无法集中精力于你想要的东西时，一切都开始了。你不再创造想要的东西，开始说这样的话：我讨厌我的工作，我的男朋友/女朋友很麻烦，我不喜欢这里，并且这样的情况一直持续下去，然后逐步恶化，而你却不知道哪里出了问题。

我知道是什么地方出了错。你无法控制你的思想，并停止创造你生活里想要的东西。

思想是力量强大的能量，它只能来自于你自己的心态。

in your life. Since your thoughts create reality, you create your reality.

Just as the conscience[1] mind is the source of thought, so the subconscience mind is the source of power. You give instructions to your subconscious mind through your thoughts. It doesn't know good from bad or right from wrong. It only follows your instructions, which are your thoughts. It will create anything you tell it.

Pay attention to your thoughts. Analyze them and listen to what you are thinking. Then decide if these are good thoughts, bad thoughts or needless thoughts. Decide if these thoughts work for you or against you.

Take control of your thoughts and make the most of[2] your life. Remember, the Bible says, "Whatsoever[3] things are true, honest, just, pure, lovely, of good report, if there be any virtue, or any praise, think on these things."

你是唯一能支配你的心态的人，你创造了思维，而思维决定你的生活环境。因为你的想法创造了现实，所以是你创造了你的现实。

正如意识是思想的源泉一样，潜意识是力量的源泉。你通过思想指导自己的潜意识。它无法辨别好与坏或对与错。它只遵循你的指示，也就是你的想法。你告诉它什么，它就创造什么。

注意你的思想。分析它们，然后倾听自己的想法。然后再决定这些是好想法、坏想法还是无用的想法。决定这些想法对你有利的还是有害的。

控制你的想法，充分利用你的生活。请记住，圣经上说："凡是事实的、庄重的、公正的、纯洁的、可爱的、声誉好的，无论是什么美德，什么称赞，这些事你们都应当思念。"

1 conscience /ˈkɒnʃns/　n.　良心，道德心
2 make the most of　充分利用
3 whatsoever /ˌwɒtsəʊˈevə/　adv.　（用于否定句中以加强语气）任何

含英咀华

　　在文章中，作者首先提出问题：我们为什么常常积极地开始一项新工作，却在完成的过程中又出现消极的情绪呢？然后作者作出了回答：是我们的思想在作怪。最后作者又提出解决问题的方法。全文结构清楚，条理分明，值得英语学习者学习和模仿。

Marilyn Manning
马瑞林·曼宁

本文的作者马瑞林·曼宁是一位心理辅导工作者，写了大量关于心理辅导方面的短文。

It's Never Too Late

Several years ago, while attending a communications course, I experienced a most unusual process. The instructor asked us to list anything in our past that we felt ashamed of, guilty about, regretted, or incomplete about. The next week he invited participants to read their lists aloud. This seemed like a very private process, but there's always some brave soul in the crowd who will volunteer[1]. As people read their lists, mine grew longer. After three weeks, I had 101 items on my list. The instructor then suggested that we find ways to make amends, apologize to people, or take some actions to right any wrongdoing. I was seriously wondering how this could ever improve my communications, having visions of alienating[2] just about everyone from my life.

The next week, the man next to me raised his hand and volunteered this story:

"While making my list, I remembered an incident from high school. I grew up in a small town in Lowa. There was a sheriff[3] in town that none of us kids liked. One night, my two buddies and I decided to play a trick on Sheriff Brown. After drinking a few beers, we found a can of red paint, climbed the tall water tank in

1 volunteer /ˌvɒlənˈtɪə/ v. 志愿
2 alienate /ˈeɪliəneɪt/ v. 使……疏远，离间
3 sheriff /ˈʃerɪf/ n. 郡治安官，州长

永远不会晚

几年前我参加一个交际课程班的时候，经历了一件非比寻常的事情。教员让我们把所有过去感到羞愧、内疚、遗憾或者是半途而废的事全部列出清单来。第二个星期，他邀请学员把清单大声读出来。这看起来是个人隐私，但人群中还是有勇敢的人自愿参加。听人们读时，我的清单更长了。三周后，我已经在清单上写下了101条。然后，教员建议我们想方设法弥补，赔礼道歉或采取某些行动来改正错误。我当时认真地想，这怎么能提高我的交际能力呢？这种情形只会让我的生命中的人都疏远自己。

又过了一周，坐在我旁边的一个人举起了手，自愿讲了一个这样的故事。

"我列清单时，想起了中学的一件小事。我在艾奥瓦州的一个小镇上长大，那里有一个治安官，我们所有的小孩儿都讨厌他。一天晚上，我和两个朋友决定好好捉弄治安官一番。我们喝了点啤酒，然后找到一罐红漆，爬上镇中心高高的蓄水池，用鲜红的大字在上面写道：治安

the middle of town, and wrote, on the tank, in bright red letters: Sheriff Brown is an s.o.b. The next day, the town arose to see our glorious sign. Within two hours, Sheriff Brown had my two pals and me in his office. My friends confessed and I lied, denying the truth. No one ever found out."

"Nearly 20 years later, Sheriff Brown's name appeared on my list. I didn't even know if he was still alive. Last weekend, I dialed information in my hometown back in Lowa. Sure enough, there was a Roger Brown still listed. I dialed his number. After a few rings, I heard: 'Hello?' I said: 'Sheriff Brown?' Pause. 'Yup.' 'Well, this is Jimmy Calkins. And I want you to know that I did it.' Pause. 'I knew it!' He yelled back. We had a good laugh and a lively discussion. His closing words were: 'Jimmy, I always felt badly for you because your buddies got it off their chest, and I knew you were carrying it around all these years. I want to thank you for calling me...for your sake.'"

Jimmy inspired me to clear up[1] all 101 items on my list. It took me almost two years, but became the springboard[2] and true inspiration for my career as a conflict mediator. No matter how difficult the conflict, crisis or situation, I always remember that it's never too late to clear up the past and begin resolution.

---

1 clear up   澄清，例如 We must try to clear up the mystery.（我们必须努力澄清这一神秘事件。）
2 springboard /'sprɪŋbɔːd/   n. 跳板

官布朗是畜生。第二天，全镇人都看到了我们的杰作。不到两个小时，我和两个朋友就被带到了他的办公室。我的两个朋友招供了，而我撒了谎，拒不承认事实，后来也没有人发现。"

"大约过了20年，我的清单上出现了治安官布朗的名字，我甚至都不知道他是否还活着。上个周末，我打电话到艾奥瓦州的家乡咨询。果然名单上还有一个叫罗杰布朗的人，于是我拨通了他的电话。电话响了几声后，我听到：'你好？'我说：'是治安官布朗吗？'他迟疑了一会儿：'是的。''哦，我是吉米·考克斯。我想让你知道我曾经做过那件事情。'他又停了一会儿。'我早就知道了'，他大声说道。我们都笑了，并欢快地聊了起来。最后他说道：'吉米，以前我总是为你难过，因为你的朋友说出了心里话，而你这些年却一直背负着它。我还很感谢你打电话给我……为了你的解脱。'"

吉米鼓励我清除清单上的101件事情。我几乎花了两年的时间。但是这件事却真正激发了我从事矛盾调解员的灵感，成为我事业的新起点。不论境况何等艰难、矛盾，我总会记得，抹去过去的阴影，踏上新的寻求之路，永远都不晚。

含英咀华

　　这篇文章在网上广泛流传，作者通过一个学员的亲身经历告诉大家要勇敢地面对自己的过失，做补救的工作，永远都不会晚。本文的最大特色就是几乎没有说理性的语言，作者只是平铺直叙，告诉了大家一个再普通不过的故事。也许每个人都会有自己遗憾的过去，但弥补遗憾的努力到什么时候都不会晚。人生是短暂的，要想活得充实、圆满，就要学会卸下心灵的包袱，与其生活在自责与悔恨中，不如勇敢地承认自己的过失，让自己的心灵得到彻底的解脱。

Benjamin Franklin

本杰明·富兰克林

本文作者简介见《哨子》。

他山之石 可以攻玉

The Handsome and Deformed Leg

美腿与丑腿

There are two types of people in the world. Although they have equal degree of health and wealth and the other comforts of life, one becomes happy, the other becomes miserable[1]. This arises from the different ways in which they consider things, persons, and events, and the resulting effects upon their minds.

In whatever situation men can be placed, they may find conveniences and inconveniences. In whatever company, they may find persons and conversations more or less pleasing. At whatever table, they may find meat and drink of better and worse taste, dishes better or worse prepared. In whatever climate, they may find good and bad weather. Under whatever government, they may find good or bad laws, and good and bad administration of these laws. In every poem or work of genius, they may see beauties and faults. In almost every face and every person, they may discover fine features and defects, good and bad qualities.

Under these circumstances, the people who are to be happy fix their attention on the conveniences of things, the pleasant parts of conversation, the well-prepared dishes, the

世界上有两种人。这两种人的健康、财富以及生活上的舒适状况大致相同，结果却是一种人快乐，另一种人痛苦。产生这种结果是由于他们对物、人和事的观点不同，而这些不同的观点对他们的思想产生了影响。

人不论身处何种境遇，都可能会觉得方便或不方便。不论在什么样的公司里，都可能会觉得周围的人以及与他们的谈话令自己愉快或不快。不论在什么样的餐桌上，都可能会觉得食物和饮料味道好或不好，菜肴烹饪得也会有好有坏。不论在什么样的气候条件下，总会遇到好的和坏的天气。不论什么样的政府执政，总会发现它的法律有好有坏，而法律的实施也会有好有坏。在天才所写的诗文里，总会发现瑕疵与优美并存。几乎在每一张脸上和每个人身上，总可以发现优点和缺点，好的品质和坏的品质。

在这些境况之中，前面提到的两种人会把他们的注意

1 miserable /ˈmɪzrəbl/ *adj.* 悲惨的，痛苦的

goodness of the wines, the fine weather. They enjoy all the cheerful things. Those who are to be unhappy think and speak only of the contrary things. Therefore, they are continually discontented themselves. By their remarks, they sour the pleasures of society, offend many people, and make themselves disagreeable everywhere. If this turn of mind were founded in nature, such unhappy persons would be the more to be pitied. The disposition[1] to criticize and be disgusted[2] is perhaps taken up originally by imitation. It grows into a habit, unknown to its possessors. The habit may be strong, but it may be cured when those who have it are convinced of its bad effects on their congeniality[3]. I hope this little admonition[4] may be of service to them, and help them change this habit. Although in fact it is chiefly an act of the imagination, it has serious consequences in life, since it brings on real grief and misfortune. These people offend many others, nobody loves them, and no one treats them with more than the most common civility[5] and respect, and scarcely than. This frequently puts them in bad humor and draws them into disputes. If they aim at obtaining some advantages in rank or fortune, nobody wishes them success. Nor will anyone stir[6] a step or speak a word

---

1 disposition /ˌdɪspəˈzɪʃn/   n.   性情
2 disgust /dɪsˈɡʌst/   v.   使厌恶
3 congeniality /kənˌdʒiːnɪˈæləti/   n.   适合，相宜
4 admonition /ˌædməˈnɪʃn/   n.   警告，劝告
5 civility /səˈvɪləti/   n.   礼貌，端庄
6 stir /stɜː/   v.   激起，惹起，搅和

力集中在不同的地方，快乐的人所注意的是事物便利的方面、谈话有趣的部分、精心烹制的菜肴、美味的佳酿、晴朗的天气等等，他们愉快地享受这一切；沮丧的人所想的和所谈的却恰恰相反。因此他们永远都不满意，他们在社交场合的言论总是令人扫兴，当面得罪了许多人，以致他们到处都不讨人喜欢。如果这种思维秉性是天生的，这些不快乐的人就更值得同情了。但这种吹毛求疵、令人厌恶的性格最初很可能是产生于模仿，然后在不知不觉中变成一种习惯。不过，当他们认识到这种坏习惯对他们一生的幸福会有多么恶劣的影响时，即使这习惯已经到了根深蒂固的程度，也还是可以改正的。我希望这一小小的忠告会对他们有些用处，帮助他们改变习惯；尽管这种坏习惯主要产生于偏见，它却会在生活中造成严重的后果，带来实实在在的悲哀与不幸。他们得罪了大家，谁也不喜欢这种人，至多以最常见的礼貌和尊敬来对待他们，有时甚至连这种礼貌和尊敬都谈不上。这往往使他们很不高兴，并常常将他们卷入驳斥和争论之中。

to favor their ambitions. If they incur[1] public censure[2] or disgrace, no one will defend or excuse them, and many will join to aggravate[3] their misconduct. These people should change this bad habit and condescend[4] to be pleased with what is pleasing, without fretting[5] themselves and others. If they do not, it can be disagreeable and sometimes very inconvenient especially when one becomes entangled[6] in their quarrels.

An old philosopher friend of mine grew very cautious from experience, and carefully avoided any contact with such people. He had a thermometer[7] to show him the temperature, and a barometer[8] to show when the weather was likely to be good or bad. Since there is no instrument, however, to discover an unpleasant disposition in a person at first sight, he made use of his legs. One of his legs was remarkably handsome, the other, by some accident, was crooked[9] and deformed. If a stranger looked at his ugly leg more than his handsome one, he doubted him. If he spoke of it and took no notice of the handsome leg, my friend had sufficient reason not to bother with him any

如果他们想要地位上升或财富增加，没有人会希望他们成功，没有人肯为他们实现愿望而出力或说话。如果他们激起民愤或当众出丑，也没有人会为他们辩护或予以原谅，许多人还会加入进来，夸大他们的错误，把他们骂得体无完肤。如果这些人不愿改掉这种坏习惯，不愿为令人愉快的事感到高兴，非要自寻烦恼或打击别人，那么大家还是避免和他们交往为好。因为这种人总是令人不快，一旦你发觉自己被牵扯进他们的争吵中，你会觉得非常麻烦。

我有一位颇有哲学头脑的老朋友因经验使然，对这种人非常小心，尽量避免与这种人交往。他用温度计测量冷暖，用晴雨表预测天气。因为还没有任何仪器能在第一眼就测出这种令人不快的性格，为此他用他的双腿作为测量工具；他一条腿完美无缺，另一条却由于某种意外事件而变得弯曲和畸形。如果一个陌生人在第一次会面中注意他的丑腿多于美腿，他会开始怀疑对方的性格。如果此人只谈及那条丑腿，而不注意那条美腿，这就足以使我的哲学家朋友决定不

他山之石　可以攻玉

---

1 incur /ɪnˈkɜː(r)/　v.　招致，蒙受，遭遇
2 censure /ˈsenʃə(r)/　n.　责难，非难
3 aggravate /ˈæɡrəveɪt/　v.　使恶化，使更严重
4 condescend /ˌkɒndɪˈsend/　v.　谦逊，屈就
5 fret /fret/　v.　烦恼，不满，磨损
6 entangle /ɪnˈtæŋɡl/　v.　使……纠缠，卷入，使……混乱
7 thermometer /θəˈmɒmɪtə(r)/　n.　温度计
8 barometer /bəˈrɒmɪtə(r)/　n.　气压计，晴雨表
9 crooked /ˈkrʊkɪd/　adj.　弯曲的，歪的，邪恶的

longer.

Not everyone has this two-legged instrument, but everyone, with a little attention, may observe signs of that kind of fault —— finding disposition and make the same resolution to avoid those infected with it. I therefore advise those critical, argumentative, discontented, unhappy people, that if they wish to be respected and loved by others, and happy in themselves, they should stop looking at the ugly leg.

再和他进一步交往下去。

并不是每个人都有这样的两条腿可作为测量人心的仪器，但是只要稍微留心，每个人都能看出一些迹象——确定谁有这种吹毛求疵的性格，从而可以避免与染上这种毛病的人交往。因此我建议那些苛刻挑剔、牢骚满腹、事事不满、郁郁寡欢的人，如果想得到他人的尊敬和喜爱并感到快乐，就不要再盯着那条丑腿了。

含英咀华

在本文中，作者告诉我们乐观积极的人受人喜爱尊敬，从而获得幸福，悲观消极的人令人生厌憎恶，因而一生不幸，希望人们摒弃消极悲观，拥有积极乐观。他把"美腿"比作优点、长处、积极的一面；用"丑腿"象征缺点、短处、消极的一面。在区分完这两种人之后，运用了排比，使得句式整齐，语言流畅有气势，强有力地说明了万事万物总有两面性。接下来作者又用朴实的语言，抽丝剥茧，层层分析，运用正反对比手法，让我们看到了乐观的好处。

Ralph Waldo Emerson
拉尔夫·沃尔多·爱默生

拉尔夫·沃尔多·爱默生(1803~1882)，近现代人类社会优秀的思想家、杰出的散文大师、美国文艺复兴的领袖。1803年出生于波士顿一个牧师家庭，从小受到良好的教育。青年时代就读于哈佛大学，毕业后曾担任神教(Unitarism)牧师，后长期从事演讲。他的许多作品，如《论自然》(Nature, 1836)、《美国学者》(The American Scholar, 1837)、《论自助》(Self-Reliance, 1841)、《代表人物》(Representative Men, 1850)、《英国人的性格》(English Traits, 1856)等，脍炙人口，赢得了无数读者的热爱。他一方面融合东西方文化，一方面打破陈规，大胆创新，提出了许许多多新的思想，极大地丰富了文艺复兴以来逐渐形成的人文主义思想。

Circles

The eye is the first circle; the horizon which it forms is the second; and throughout nature this primary picture is repeated without end. It is the highest emblem[1] in the cipher of the world. St. Augustine[2] described the nature of God as a circle whose centre was everywhere and its circumference[3] nowhere. We are all our lifetime reading the copious sense of this first of forms. One moral we have already deduced in considering the circular or compensatory[4] character of every human action. Another analogy we shall now trace, that every action admits of being outdone. Our life is an apprenticeship[5] to the truth that around every circle another can be drawn; that there is no end in nature, but every end is a beginning; that there is always another dawn risen on mid-noon, and under every deep a lower deep opens.

This fact, as far as it symbolizes the moral fact of the Unattainable, the flying Perfect, around which the hands of man can never meet, at once the inspirer and the condemner of every

---

1 emblem /ˈembləm/ n. 象征，标志
2 St. Augustine: 圣·奥古斯丁（354~430），生活于罗马帝国走向衰落的年代，是当时最伟大的神学家，其《上帝之城》（The City of God）等神学著作在整个中世纪对基督教的学说和观点影响深远
3 circumference /səˈkʌmfərəns/ n. 圆周
4 compensatory /ˌkɒmpenˈseɪtəri/ adj. 补偿的，报酬的
5 apprenticeship /əˈprentɪʃɪp/ n. 学徒身份的期限

论圆

眼睛是第一个圆，眼前的地平线是第二个圆。这个原始的形状在自然界中到处都是，没有止境。圆是一种最高形式的象征。圣·奥古斯丁把圆作为对上帝本质的描述，它有着无所不在的圆心，但是其圆周却无处可寻。我们用一生的时间来理解这个最原始的图形有什么丰富内涵。在讨论人类每一个行为的循环及其补偿性时，我们从中探寻出了一种道德。我们要研究的另一个类比是：每种行为都能够被超越。有这样一条真理贯穿在我们的生活当中，即：在任何一个圆的外围都可以画出另外一个圆；自然没有极限，每个终点都是一个新的起点；太阳爬到最高处时，总会有另一道曙光冉冉升起；深海处还有更深的海床。

这一事实象征着"难以企及"的道德事实，即转眼即逝的"完善"，由于人类的双手不可能绕过这种完善而再度合拢，既鼓舞又谴责成功，从这一点来说，圆则可以帮助我们把人类在各个方面显示出来的力量结合起来。

success, may conveniently serve us to connect many illustrations of human power in every department.[1]

There are no fixtures in nature. The universe is fluid and volatile[2]. Permanence is but a word of degrees. Our globe seen by God is a transparent law, not a mass of facts. The law dissolves[3] the fact and holds it fluid. Our culture is the predominance of an idea which draws after it all this train of cities and institutions. Let us rise into another idea; they will disappear. The Greek sculpture is all melted away, as if it had been statues of ice: here and there a solitary figure or fragment remaining, as we see flecks and scraps of snow left in cold dells and mountain clefts in June and July. For the genius that created it creates now somewhat else. The Greek letters last a little longer, but are already passing under the same sentence and tumbling into the inevitable pit which the creation of new thought opens for all that is old.[4] The new continents are built out of the ruins of an old planet; the new races fed out of the decomposition of the foregoing. New arts destroy the old. See the investment of capital in aqueducts[5], made useless by hydraulics[6];

---

1 本句话的主句是 "This fact may conveniently serve us to connect many illustrations of human power in every department"；as far as...succeess 是条件状语；around which...是非限制性定语从句，修饰 the Unattainable, the flying Perfect
2 volatile /'vɒlətaɪl/ adj. 可变的，不稳定的
3 dissolve /dɪ'zɒlv/ vt. 溶解
4 "which the creation of new thought opens for all that is old" 是定语从句套另一个定语从句，which 所引导的定语从句修饰 pit；that is old 是定语从句修饰 all
5 aqueduct /'ækwɪdʌkt/ n. 沟渠，导水管
6 hydraulics /haɪ'drɔːlɪks/ n. 水力学

自然界的任何事物都不是永恒不变的。宇宙是运动变化的。"永恒"只是一个表示不同程度的概念。在上帝的眼中，我们的星球是一则透明的法规，而不是事实的累积。事实因为溶解在法规中而运转。我们的文化不过是一种占据支配地位的理念，它黏附着一套城市和机构。只要我们的理念转变了，它们就会随之消亡。古希腊的雕刻早已不复存在，像冰雕一样消逝，只剩下一些零星孤独的碎片，好似六七月间阴谷的石缝中零零散散的残雪。因为开辟新事物的天才又创造了另外的东西。希腊字母流传得更久远一些，但也同样避免不了要遭受厄运，最终掉进新思想为所有的旧思想设置的不可逆转的深渊里。新大陆是在这个古老星球的废墟上建立的；新物种是在前代腐化的尸体上孕育的；新艺术占据了旧艺术的地位。人们原来发明的导水管，由于后来出现的液压传动而成为废品；防御工事在火药面前脆弱得不堪一击；铁路的发明让公路和运河相形见绌；蒸汽机取代了船帆；随即电动机又应时而生。

fortifications, by gunpowder; roads and canals, by railways; sails, by steam; steam, by electricity.

Valor consists in the power of self-recovery, so that a man cannot have his flank turned, cannot be out-general led, but put him where you will, he stands. This can only be by his preferring truth to his past apprehension of truth, and his alert acceptance of it from whatever quarter; the intrepid[1] conviction that his laws, his relations to society, his Christianity, his world, may at any time be superseded and decease.

The difference between talents and character is adroitness[2] to keep the old and trodden round, and power and courage to make a new road to new and better goals. Character makes an overpowering present, a cheerful, determined hour, which fortifies all the company by making them see that much is possible and excellent that was not thought of.[3] Character dulls the impression of particular events. When we see the conqueror we do not think much of any one battle or success. We see that we had exaggerated the difficulty. It was easy to him. The great man is not convulsible or tormentable. He is so much that events pass over him without much impression. People say sometimes, "See what I have overcome; see how cheerful I am; see how completely I have triumphed over these

---

1 intrepid /ɪnˈtrepɪd/ *adj.* 勇猛的，坚忍不拔的，无畏的
2 adroitness /əˈdrɔɪtnɪs/ *n.* 熟练，灵巧，机灵
3 "which...was not though of" 是非限制性定语从句，修饰 hour；"that was not thought of" 是定语从句，修饰 much

勇气在于有很强的自我重塑能力，只有这样，一个人才能永远立于不败之地，才能不受人摆布；不管你把他放在什么场合，他都有立足之地。要想做到这一点，他就必须选择真理，摒弃他对真理原有的理解，能够从不同的角度认识接受真理，而且要相信他的法律条文、他与社会之间的联系、他的宗教、他的世界随时都有可能被取代而消逝。

天才与杰出人物的区别在于，杰出人物灵活地保存了旧有的、被人批判了的事物，同时又有能力开辟新的道路，建立新的目标。杰出人物创造压倒一切的现时，一种愉快而坚定的时刻，他树立起坚定的信念展现给世人，他让他们看到，他们没有想过的很多很多事情其实都可以实现，而且可以做得很优秀。杰出人物让事件本身在人们的印象中淡化。当我们见到征服者时，他们创造的某次战役或胜利倒不会过多地在我们的头脑中被想象。我们只知道，原来我们把困难夸大了。我们的困难对于伟人而言其实很容易。伟人是坚定不可动摇的。在他眼中，任何事情都是过眼烟云，不会留下什么不可磨灭的印象。有时候人们会说："看，我已经克服了困难，瞧我

black events." Not if they still remind me of the black evens — they have not yet conquered. Is it conquest to be a gay and decorated sepulcher, or a half-crazed widow, hysterically laughing? True conquest is the causing the black event to fade and disappear as an early cloud of insignificant result in a history so large and advancing.

The one thing which we seek with insatiable[1] desire is to forget ourselves, to be surprised out of our propriety, to lose our semidiurnal[2] memory and to do something without knowing how or why; in short to draw a new circle. Nothing great was ever achieved without enthusiasm. The way of life is wonderful. It is by abandonment. The great moments of history are the facilities of performance through the strength of ideas, as the works of genius and religion. "A man," said Oliver Cromwell, "never rises so high as when he knows not whither he is going." Dreams and drunkenness, the use of opium and alcohol are the semblance[3] and counterfeit of this oracular genius, and hence their dangerous attraction for men. For the like reason they ask the aid of wild passions, as in gaming and war, to ape in some manner these flames and generosities of the heart.

多开心呀！我已经彻底战胜这些磨难了。"可是如果他们反复地对我说起那厄运，就说明他们还没有打败它。试问，一个装饰得色彩鲜艳的坟墓，或一个歇斯底里大笑的半疯寡妇，算得上征服者吗？淡化磨难才是真正的胜利，并随之让它犹如缥缈的晨雾一样消失在无边无际、不断发展的历史中。

我们不断追求的是忘我的境界，走出自得其乐的圈子，失去恒久的记忆，全身心地投入做某件事情，简单地说来，就是重新画一个圆。没有热情就不会有所成就。生活是精彩的，精彩来自于放弃。历史上的伟大时刻都是借助了强有力的思想得以展现的，比如天才和宗教著作。克伦·威尔曾经说过："当一个人不再受固于某个限定的去向时，他就可以登峰造极了。"也正是因为这样，梦境、黑暗、陶醉沉迷于鸦片和酒精等酷似神仙的感觉才会对人们构成致命的诱惑。同样的道理，人们追求狂热情感的辅助如同在比赛和战争中一样，借此来模拟心灵的热烈与宽宏大量。

1 insatiable /ɪnˈseɪʃəbl/ adj. 不知足的，贪得无厌的
2 semidiurnal /ˌsemɪdaɪˈɜːnl/ adj. 半天的，一天两次的
3 semblance /ˈsembləns/ n. 外表，样子

含英咀华

在《论圆》这篇文章中，爱默生作了充分的展开：事物就是无数的圆，围绕一个圆可以再画一个圆。人生也是如此，从一个小得看不见的圆圈开始，向四面八方扩散，涌现出一个个新的越来越大的圆，而且永远没有止境。《论圆》充分体现了爱默生坚信个体具有无限发展潜力的乐观思想。

John Henry Bradley

约翰·亨利·布莱德利

约翰·亨利·布莱德利（1815～1870），十九世纪美国著名的专栏作家、评论家、文学家，著有散文集及新闻专著若干。

Hour in the Sun

"I was rich, if not in money, in sunny hours and summer days." When Thoreau wrote that line, he was thinking of the Walden. Pond he knew as a boy.

Woodchoppers[1] and the Iron Horse had not yet greatly damaged the beauty of its setting. A boy could go to the pond and lie on his back against the seat of a boat, lazily drifting from shore to shore while the loons dived and the swallows dipped around him. Thoreau loved to recall such sunny hours and summer days when "idleness[2] was the most attractive and productive business."

I too was a boy in love with a pond, rich in sunny hours and summer days. Sun and summer are still what the always were, but the boy and the pond changed. The boy, who is now a man, no longer finds much time for idle drifting. The pond has been annexed[3] by a great city. The swamps where herons once hunted are now drained and filled with houses .The bay where water lilies quietly floated is now a harbor for motor boats. In short, everything that the boy loved no longer exists— except in the man's memory of it.

Some people insist that only today and

---

1 woodchopper /ˈwʊdtʃɒpə(r)/ n. 伐木者
2 idleness /ˈaɪdlnəs/ n. 无所事事，浪费时间
3 annex /əˈneks/ v. 吞并

阳光下的时光

"我是富足的，即使没有万贯家资，却也拥有无数个艳阳天与夏日。"当梭罗写下这句话时，他在怀念儿时的瓦尔登湖。

那时，伐木者与火车还未严重破坏湖畔美丽的景色。小男孩可以来到湖边，仰卧于小舟之中，悠闲地在两岸之间漂流。在他周围，潜水鸟在戏水，还有燕子轻盈地掠过湖面。梭罗喜欢回忆这样的艳阳天与夏日，此时，"悠闲是最具有魅力且颇有裨益的事情"。

我曾经也是个热爱湖泊的小男孩，也拥有无数个艳阳天与夏日。阳光与夏日依旧，而小男孩与湖泊却已改变。小男孩已长大成人，再也没有时间去漂游。而湖泊却被大城市吞并。苍鹭曾经觅食的沼泽早已干涸，上面盖满了房舍。睡莲漂浮的湖湾，也成了汽艇停泊的港口。总之，小男孩所喜爱的都已不复存在——一切只停留在他的记忆里。

一些人坚持认为只有今日与明日最重要。可要按这条规

他山之石 可以攻玉

tomorrow matter[1]. But how much poorer we would be if we really lived by that rule! So much of what we do today is frivolous[2] and futile and soon forgotten. So much of what we hope to do tomorrow never happens.

The past is the bank in which we store our most valuable possession: the memories that give meaning and depth to our lives. Those who truly treasure the past will not bemoan[3] the passing of the good old days, because days enshrined in memory are never lost. Death itself is powerless to still a remembered voice or erase a remembered smile. And for one boy who is now a man, there is a pond which neither time nor tide can change, where he can still spend a quiet hour in the sun.

则来生活的话，我们的生活将会变得更加贫瘠。今天我们所做之事有多少是琐碎无功的，很快就会被人遗忘。又有多少我们明天要为之事将会成为泡影。

过去是一所银行，我们将最珍贵的财富——记忆——珍藏其中。这些记忆赋予我们生命的意义和厚度。真正珍惜过去之人不会为美好时光的逝去而哀叹，因为那些珍藏于记忆中的时光是永远不会消失的。就连死亡也无法改变记忆中的声音，或抹去记忆中的微笑。对于已经长大成人的小男孩来说，总有一个池塘不会因时间和潮汐而改变，在那里他可以继续在阳光下享受静谧的时光。

---

1 matter /'mætə(r)/ v. 要紧
2 frivolous /'frɪvələs/ adj. 无聊的，漫不经心的
3 bemoan /bɪ'məʊn/ v. 抱怨

含英咀华

　　本文是布莱德利流传最广的经典之作，作者用细腻的手法和朴实无华的语言告诉我们记忆赋予我们生命的意义和厚度，虽然时间匆匆，但我们也要适时停下脚步回忆一下美好的过去，才能更有动力前进。而且，作者标新立异，将"过去"比作"银行"，"银行的存款"既是我们对过去的积累，也是我们未来的保障，正如那句流传已久的话，"忘记过去就意味着背叛"。所以，当你读过本文之后，请停下匆匆的脚步，去寻找你曾失落的美好回忆，去好好享受一下灿烂的阳光。

锲而不舍
金石可镂

James Allen
詹姆士·艾伦

詹姆士·艾伦(1864~1912)，英格兰著名作家，被誉为"人生哲学之父"。他出生于英格兰的一个富商家庭，由于家境的逆转使他不得不在15岁的时候离开学校。但是，他内心深处始终没有放弃对理想的追求，直到1902年，他毅然辞去了工作，和妻子一起搬到英格兰西南部海边的小农庄。在那里艾伦受自己的心灵导师——托尔斯泰的启发，过着一种清贫、自律的简单生活，直到去世。期间，他一共写了包括《我的人生思考》(As a Man Thinketh, 1902)等19本书。他的真知灼见丰沛如泉，激励鼓舞了一代又一代的读者，焕发出永久的生命力。

The Glorious Conquest

Truth can only be apprehended by the conquest of self. Blessedness can only be arrived at by overcoming the lower nature. The way of Truth is barred by a man's self. The only enemies that can actually hinder him are his own passions and delusions[1]. Until a man realizes this, and commences to cleanse his heart, he has not found the Path which leads to knowledge and peace. Until passion is transcended[2], Truth remains unknown. This is the Divine Law.

A man cannot keep his passions and have Truth as well. Error is not slain until selfishness is dead. The overcoming of self is no mystical theory, but a very real and practical thing. It is a process which must be pursued daily and hourly, with unswerving[3] faith and undaunted resolution if any measure of success is to be achieved.

The process is one of orderly growth, having its sequential stages, like the growth of a tree; and as fruit can only be produced by carefully and patiently training the tree even so the pure and satisfying fruits of holiness can only be obtained by faithfully and patiently training the

1 delusion /dɪˈluːʒn/ *n.* 错觉
2 transcend /trænˈsend/ *v.* 超越，胜过
3 unswerving /ʌnˈswɜːvɪŋ/ *adj.* 坚定的，不改变的

光荣的征服

只有成功征服自我的人，才能掌握真理。只有克服了低劣天性的人，才能得到幸福。一个人的自私，就是他通往真理之路的障碍。真正能够阻得他的唯一敌人，就是自己的激情和错觉。只有当一个人意识到这一点，并开始净化自己的心灵时，他才会找到通往知识与和平的道路。一个人只有超越自己的激情，才会懂得真理。这是神圣的规律。

一个人不可能同时保持激情并拥有真理。只有消灭自私，错误才会不复存在。自我征服并不是什么神圣的理论，而是一件非常真实和实际的事情。这是一个必须每日每时去坚持的过程，只要有坚定不移的信念和勇敢无畏的决心，就能掌握获得成功的方法。

这个过程是一种有规律的成长，它有自己连续的阶段，就像一棵树的成长一样；只有在对树的细致精心的照料下，才能结出果实，同理，在正确思想和行为的成长过程中，只有对心灵加以忠实耐心的培养，才会得到纯洁的、令人满

mind in the growth of right thought and conduct.

There are five steps in the overcoming of passion (which includes all bad habits and particular forms of wrong-doing) which I will call:

Repression

Endurance

Elimination

Understanding

Victory

When men fail to overcome their sins, it is because they try to begin at the wrong end. They want to have the stage of Victory without passing through the previous four stages. They are in the position of a gardener who wants to produce good fruit without training and attending to his trees. Repression consists in checking and controlling the wrong act (such as an outburst of temper, a hasty or unkind word, a selfish indulgence etc.), and not allowing it to take actual form. This is equivalent to the gardener nipping off the useless buds and branches from his tree. It is a necessary process, but a painful one. The tree bleeds while undergoing the process and the gardener knows that it must not be taxed too severely. The heart also bleeds when it refuses to return passion for passion, when it ceases to defend and justify itself. It is the process of "mortifying the members" of which St. Paul speaks.

But this repression is only the beginning of

意的果实。

克服激情分五个步骤（这里所说的激情包括所有恶习和产生错误行为的个性），我称它们为：

抑制

忍耐

消除

理解

胜利。

如果人们无法克服自己的罪恶，那是因为他们试图以错误的目标开始。他们想不经过前面四个步骤就直接到达胜利的阶段。就像不去培育照料树木，却想得到果实的园丁。抑制存在于对错误行为（例如生气，随意刻薄的话语，自私的放纵等）的检查和控制中，并且不会让这种错误行为真实发生。这就相当于园丁检查树上无用的嫩芽和树枝一样。这是一个必需的过程，但也是一个痛苦的过程。在这期间，树木会受伤，而园丁知道不能给它太重的负担。当心灵不能以激情回报激情，当心灵停止防御和证明自己时，它自己也会流血。这就是圣·保罗所说的"苦修"的过程。

然而，这种抑制仅仅是自我征服的开始。如果他自行

self-conquest. When it is made an end in itself, and there is no object of finally purifying the heart, that is a stage of hypocrisy[1]; a hiding of one's true nature, and striving to appear better in the eyes of others than one really is. In that case it is an evil, but when adopted as the first stage toward complete purification[2], it is good. Its practice leads to the second stage of Endurance, or forbearance, in which one silently endures the pain which arises in the mind when it is brought in contact with certain actions and attitudes of other minds toward one. As success is attained[3] in this stage, the striver comes to see that all his pain actually arises in his own weaknesses, and not in the wrong attitudes of others toward him, these latter being merely the means by which his sins are brought to the surface and revealed to him. He thus gradually exonerates[4] all others from blame in his falls and lapses of conduct, and accuses only himself, and so learns to love those who thus unconsciously reveal to him his sins and shortcomings.

Having passed through these two stages of self-crucifixion[5], the disciple enters the third, that of Elimination, in which the wrong thought which lay behind the wrong

终止此过程，并且没有最终净化心灵的目标，说明那只是一个虚伪的阶段；只不过是隐藏起真实的本性，并试图以优于真实面貌的假象出现在他人眼里。如果是那样的话，那就是错误的，但如果以彻底的净化作为第一阶段，那就是正确的。通过这一过程，会使人迈向第二阶段——忍耐，或是克制；在这个阶段，当他受到别人不公平的对待时，会默默忍受思想中出现的痛苦。当在这一阶段取得成功时，这个努力奋斗过的人就会明白，所有的痛苦其实都是自己的软弱所致，而不是由于别人对待他的错误态度，后者只是将他错误的一面揭露出来并展示给他看而已。因而，他会逐渐明白，别人指责他的堕落行为是没有错的，他还会谴责自己，并因此学会去尊敬那些无意中揭示出他的错误和缺点的人。

经过这两个自我磨炼的阶段后，这个信徒就进入了第三个阶段——消除；在这个阶段，隐藏在错误行为后面的

---

1 hypocrisy /hɪˈpɒkrəsi/ n. 伪善
2 but ... purification: 是非谓语动词的形式，做状语
3 attain /əˈteɪn/ v. 达到，获得，完成
4 exonerate /ɪgˈzɒnəreɪt/ v. 免除责任
5 crucifixion /ˌkruːsəˈfɪkʃn/ n. 刑罪

act is cast from the mind immediately it appears. At this stage, conscious strength and holy joy begin to take the place of pain, and the mind having become comparatively calm, the striver is enabled to gain a deeper insight into the complexities of his mind, and thus to understand the inception, growth, and outworking of sin. This is the stage of Understanding.

Perfection[1] in understanding leads to the final conquest of self, a conquest so complete that the sin can no more rise in the mind even as a thought or impression; for when the knowledge of sin is complete; when it is known in its totality, from its inception as a seed in the mind to its ripened outgrowth as act and consequence, then it can no more be allowed a place in life, but it is abandoned for ever. Then the mind is at peace. The wrong acts of others no longer arouse wrong and pain in the mind of the disciple. He is glad and calm and wise. He is filled with Love, and blessedness abides with him. And this is Victory!

错误思想一出现就被摒弃。此时，自觉的力量和神圣的欢乐开始取代痛苦，思想已经变得非常平静，这个人已经能够更深入地洞察自己思想的复杂性，并因此明白了罪恶的开端、成长过程和外部表现。这就是理解的阶段。

完美的理解会带来最终对自我的征服，这种征服是如此彻底，以致思想中不再出现罪恶，即使是一个邪恶的想法或印象也不会出现；因为当对罪恶有了彻底的了解时——当它最初作为思想中的一颗种子，直到结出成熟的恶果被完全了解时——就不会再让它存在于自己的生活中，并永远将其摒弃。然后，思想就处于和平状态；他人的错误行为也不会在这个信徒的思想中引起错误和痛苦。他喜悦、和平、明智；他的心中充满了爱，幸福也伴随着他。这就是胜利！

1 perfection /pə'fekʃn/　*n.*　完善；完美

含英咀华

　　在本文中，作者用充满激情的话语告诉读者人无完人，我们的成长过程就是一个征服自我的过程，要想成功就得勇于挑战自我，完善自我。文章列举了自我征服的五个阶段，以及每个阶段之间的关系，完成每个阶段所要遇到的困难和所得到的收获，在论述的过程中，作者运用了大量的比喻使文章形象、生动、丰富。

Og Mandino
奥格·曼狄诺

奥格·曼狄诺（1923~1996），伟大的成功学大师。其作品以《世界上最伟大的推销员》(The Greatest Salesman in the World, 1968)为代表。他的著作被翻译成二十种语言，来自各行各业成千上万的人都认为奥格·曼狄诺改变了他们的人生，并让他们在书中看到了奇迹。他的书中处处充满了希望、勇气、毅力和快乐。本文就选自《世界上最伟大的推销员》，这是一本教会我们积极进取、坚持不懈、同时也保持平和心态的书。

I Will Persist Until I Succeed

坚持不懈直到成功

In the Orient young bulls are tested for the fight arena in a certain manner. Each is brought to the ring and allowed to attack a picador[1] who pricks them with a lance. The bravery of each bull is then rated with care according to the number of times he demonstrates his willingness to charge in spite of the sting of the blade. Henceforth will I recognize that each day I am tested by life in alike manner. If I persist, if I continue to try, if I continue to charge forward, I will succeed.

I will persist until I succeed.

I was not delivered unto this world in defeat, nor does failure course in my veins. I am not a sheep waiting to be prodded by my shepherd. I am a lion and I refuse to talk, to walk, to sleep with the sheep. I will not hear those who weep and complain, for their disease is contagious[2]. Let them join the sheep. The slaughterhouse of failure is not my destiny.

I will persist until I succeed.

The prizes of life are at the end of each journey, not near the beginning; and it is not given to me to know how many steps are necessary in order to reach my goal. Failure I

在古老的东方，挑选小公牛在竞技场格斗有一定的程序。它们被带进场地，向手持长矛的斗牛士进攻，裁判以它受激后再向斗牛士进攻的次数多寡来评定这只公牛的勇敢程度。从今往后，我须承认，我的生命每天都在接受类似的考验。如果我坚忍不拔，不断尝试，那么我一定会成功。

坚持不懈，直到成功。

我不是为了失败才来到这个世界上的，我的血管里也没有失败的血液在流动。我不是任人鞭打的羔羊。我是猛狮，不与羊群一起交谈、走路，甚至连睡觉都不会和它们一起。我不想听失意者的哭泣、抱怨者的牢骚，因为这些是具有传染性的。失败者的屠宰场不是我命运的归宿。

坚持不懈，直到成功。

生命的奖赏远在旅途终点，而非起点附近；我不知道要走多少步才能达到目标。踏

---

1 picador /ˈpɪkədɔː/ n. 骑马斗牛士
2 contagious /kənˈteɪdʒəs/ adj. 传染性的，会蔓延的

may still encounter at the thousandth step, yet success hides behind the next bend in the road. Never will I know how close it lies unless I turn the corner.

Always will I take another step. If that is of no avail[1], I will take another, and yet another. In truth, one step at a time is not too difficult.

I will persist until I succeed.

Henceforth, I will consider each day's effort as but one blow of my blade against a mighty oak. The first blow may cause not a tumor in the wood, nor the second, not the third. Each blows, of itself, may be trifling, and seem of no consequence, yet from childish swipes the oak will eventually tumbles. So it will be with my efforts of today.

I will be like the rain drop which washes away the mountain; the ant who devours[2] a tiger; the star which brightens the earth; the slave who builds a pyramid. I will build my castle one brick at a time for I know that small attempts, repeated, will complete any undertaking.

I will persist until I succeed.

I will never consider defeat and I will remove from my vocabulary such words and phrases as quit, cannot, unable, impossible, out of the question, improbable, failure, unworkable, hopeless, and retreat; for they are the words of fools. I will avoid despair but if this disease of the mind should infect me then I will work on in despair. I will toil and I will endure. I will ignore

上第一千步的时候，我仍然可能遭到失败，但成功就藏在拐角后面。除非拐了弯，我永远不知道成功还有多远。

再前进一步，如果没有用，就再向前一步。事实上，每次进步一点点并不太难。

坚持不懈，直到成功。

从今往后，我承认每天的奋斗就像对参天大树的一次砍击，头几刀可能了无痕迹。每一击仿佛微不足道，然而，累积起来，巨树终会倒下。这恰如我今天的努力。

我就像冲洗高山的雨滴，吞噬猛虎的蚂蚁，照亮大地的星辰，建起金字塔的奴隶。我要一砖一瓦地建造起自己的城堡，因为我深知水滴石穿的道理，只要持之以恒，什么都可以做到。

坚持不懈，直到成功。

我绝不会考虑失败，我的字典里不再有放弃、不可能、没能力、办不到、没法子、成问题、失败、行不通、没希望、退缩这类愚蠢的字眼。我要尽量避免绝望，即使真的受到它的威胁，也要在绝望中继续战

---

1 avail /əˈveɪl/ n. 没有什么效果；不成功
2 devour /dɪˈvaʊə(r)/ v. 吞食

the obstacles at my feet and keep my eyes on the goals above my head, for I know that where dry desert ends, green grass grows.

I will persist until I succeed.

I will remember the ancient law of averages and I will bend it to my good. I will persist with knowledge that each failure to sell will increase my chance for success at the next attempt. Each nay I hear will bring me closer to the sound of yea. Each frown I meet only prepares me for the smile to come. Each misfortune I encounter will carry in it the seed of tomorrow's good luck. I must have the night to appreciate the day. I must fail often to succeed only once.

I will persist until I succeed.

I will try, and try, and try again. Each obstacle I will consider as a mere detour[1] to my goal and a challenge to my profession. I will persist and develop my skills as the mariner develops his, by learning to ride out the wrath of each storm.

I will persist until I succeed.

Henceforth, I will learn and apply another secret of those who excel in my work. When each day is ended, not regarding whether it has been a success or a failure, I will attempt to achieve one more sale. When my thoughts beckon[2] my tired body homeward I will resist the temptation to depart. I will try again. I will make one more

斗。我要辛勤耕耘，忍受苦楚。我放眼未来，不再理会脚下的障碍，因为我坚信，沙漠尽头必是绿洲。

坚持不懈，直到成功。

我要牢牢记住古老的平衡法则，鼓励自己坚持下去。因为每一次的失败都会增加下一次成功的机会。每一次的否决都让我离赞成更近，每一次皱起的眉头是为将要到来的笑容做准备。每一次的不幸，往往预示着明天的好运。夜幕降临，回想一天的遭遇，我总是心存感激。我深知，只有失败多次，才能成功。

坚持不懈，直到成功。

我要尝试，尝试，再尝试。每个障碍，我都将视为通往我成功的一次小小的绕行和对我宣言的一次挑衅。我会坚持不渝熟练我的技艺，我要像水手一样，乘风破浪。

坚持不懈，直到成功。

从今往后，我要借鉴别人成功的秘诀。过去的是非成败，我全不计较，只抱定信念，明天会更好。当我筋疲力尽时，我要抵制回家的诱惑。我要再试一次。我要多试一

---

1 detour /ˈdiːtʊə(r)/   n.   绕行的路；迂回路
2 beckon /ˈbekən/   v.   招手

attempt to close with victory, and if that fails I will make another. Never will I allow any day to end with a failure. Thus will I plant the seed of tomorrow's success and gain an insurmountable[1] advantage over those who cease their labor at a prescribed time. When others cease their struggle, the mine will begin, and my harvest will be full.

I will persist until I succeed.

Nor will I allow yesterday's success to lull me into today's complacency, for this is the great foundation of failure. I will forget the happenings of the day that is gone, whether they were good or bad, and greet the new sun with confidence that this will be the best day of my life. So long as there is breath in me, that long will I persist. For now I know one of the greatest principles of success: if I persist long enough I will win.

I will persist.

I will win.

次，以接近成功，如果失败了，那我将再试一次。每一天都避免以失败收场。我要为明天的成功播种，超过那些按部就班的人。在别人停滞不前时，我继续拼搏，终有一天我会丰收!

坚持不懈，直到成功。

我不会因昨日的成功而满足，因为这是失败的先兆。我要忘却已逝昨日的一切，无论是好还是坏。我会信心百倍，迎接新的太阳，相信这是我生命中最好的一天。只要我一息尚存，就要坚持到底。因为我已深知成功的秘诀：只要坚持就能成功。

坚持不懈，
直到成功。

---

1 insurmountable /ˌɪnsə'maʊntəbl/ *adj.* 不能克服的，难以对付的

含英咀华

在本文中，作者首先以在角斗场上的公牛为例，告诉读者坚持的力量；然后又将自己比作伐木者、雨滴、蚂蚁等，来说明"有志者，事竟成"和"水滴石穿"的道理；最后又激励读者不要满足现状，要积极进取。全文文字激昂，灵活运用比喻、拟人、反复等修辞方法，给人以深刻印象，尤其是"I will persist until I succeed"的反复出现，好似一个警钟，不断敲打读者的心灵，又似一个马鞭，仿佛让人不得不坚持，不得不前行。

Ulla Sebastian
优拉·塞瓦斯蒂安

优拉·塞瓦斯蒂安博士是一位著名的作家、教育家和心理治疗师。她的大部分作品都是关于如何获取事业成功和个人成长的经历，还有心理疏导的方法等。

Ready for Success?

It is not by accident who resides on the sunny side[1] and who on the shadow side of the street. You find the key to success in what you think all day.

If your thoughts focus on abundance[2], love and integrity in your actions, this inner state manifests as success in the outer world. If you feel bogged[3] down with worries, failures or fear of the future, you draw misfortune and failure towards you.

Transactional analysis[4] tells us that winner or failure scripts are a combination of imprints[5], conditions and learned behavior. The good news is: They are not a destiny but you can change them. Thanks to Abraham Maslow and other pioneers in the field of transpersonal and quantum[6] psychology we got some good ideas of what distinguishes successful people from those who feel like being the victims of the circumstances.

Successful people influence and shape reality according to their own needs instead of letting the "facts" of life determine their fate.

准备好成功了吗?

谁属于乐观派，谁是悲观派，这绝不是偶然的。你会在每天的所思所想中发现成功的钥匙。

如果你的思考重点放在你的行为的丰富、热爱和忠诚等方面，这种内心的状态就预示了外部世界的成功。如果你陷入担心、失败或对未来的恐惧中，你就会走向不幸和失败。

人与人关系的心理分析告诉我们，成功或失败的版本是印象、条件和所学到的行为的结合。好消息是：它们不是一种宿命，你可以改变它们。多亏亚伯拉罕·马斯洛和其他先驱者在超个人和量子心理学领域的贡献，我们知道了如何区别成功的人和自感怀才不遇的那些人。

成功人士根据自己的需要影响和塑造现实，而不是让生活的"事实"决定他们的命运。

---

1 **on the sunny side:** 乐观的
2 **abundance** /əˈbʌndəns/ *n.* 丰富，充裕
3 **bog** /bɒg/ *v.* 使……陷于泥沼
4 **transactional analysis** /trænˈzækʃn//əˈnæləsɪs/ 人与人关系的心理分析
5 **imprint** /ˈɪmprɪnt/ *n.* 印记
6 **quantum** /ˈkwɒntəm/ *n.* 量子

Successful people are creators, not victims of the circumstances. Their attitudes, thoughts and actions are open for the new and flexible enough to respond to the unexpected.

Successful people do not have problems but challenges that need to be resolved. Those challenges activate[1] and inspire all their talents and resources while the concept of problems leads to worrying and being bogged down by the forces of life.

In order to access and use your full potential you need physical and inner strength. Many people know what is good for them but they do not have the self-discipline to let go of[2] bad habits and to establish good habits.

Successful people work a lot, not out of duty or greed but because they feel inspired by their own vision and mission in life.

Successful people distinguish themselves in central aspects from those with a failure script. They take 100% responsibility for their lives, focus their attention on the positive, let go of what does not serve them any longer and invite others to participate in their success. They know that it is the power and purity of their thoughts, values and attitudes that create their personal individual success, abundance and joy.

You can shift your perspective from being a

成功的人是创造者，而不是命运的受害者。他们的态度、想法和行动具有足够的新颖性和灵活性以应对意想不到的一切。

成功的人需要解决的不是问题而是挑战。挑战可以刺激和激发他们所有的才智和资源，而问题则会导致担忧和陷入生活压力的困境。

为了获取和利用你的全部潜力，你需要身体和心理的力量。很多人知道什么对他们有好处，但他们没有足够的自律意识去克服坏习惯，并建立良好的习惯。

成功人士努力工作，不是出于责任或贪婪，而是因为他们受到生活中理想和使命的鼓舞。

成功的人在主要的方面将自己和失败的人区分开。他们对自己的生活百分之百负责，把注意力集中在积极的方面，不再关注无助于他们成功的一切，并邀请他人参与其中以取得成功。他们知道是他们思想、价值观和态度的力量和纯洁性促成了他们的成功、富足与喜悦。

你可以把你的前景从一个

---

1 activate /ˈæktɪveɪt/ v. 刺激
2 let go of: 松手放开，例如 Let go of me, you vicious monster! （放开我，这可恶的家伙！）

victim to being a creator. You can move from the shadow to the sunny side of the street.

To get there you need to shift your resonance with "failure" scripts to resonate with success scripts.

How to do this? Unique tools to counter those negative thoughts are positive affirmations. If you get up in the morning thinking "another rotten day", your day will turn out quite differently, than when you get up thinking: Another exciting day for wonderful experiences! You meet the reality outside that you first create in your mind.

Positive affirmations directly affect your conscious and subconscious[1] mind.

To use them effectively, follow three basic guidelines.

1. Base your affirmations on clear, rational assessments of facts and not on a dream world. If you are struggling with getting your basic needs met, an affirmation stating: "I effortlessly meet my basic needs" will be much more effective than a statement: "I am a millionaire", although people who made it to that stage usually make good use of positive affirmations.

2. State your affirmations in the present tense so that your mind knows that what you want to achieve is already happening. Present tense means: "I have now" instead of "I would like to have" in some distant future.

3. Use positive words in your affirmations. An affirmation saying: "I am happy and content"

---

1 subconscious /ˌsʌbˈkɒnʃəs/ *adj.* 潜意识的

受害者变成一个创造者。你可以从一个悲观者变成一个乐观者。

要达到此目的你需要转移目标，不再与"失败"剧本共鸣，而是与成功剧本共鸣。

如何做到这一点？对付那些负面想法的唯一工具就是积极的断言。如果你在早晨起来就想"又是糟糕的一天"而不是想"又是充满美妙的经历令人兴奋的一天！"，你的一天会变得相当不同。你遇到的外部现实首先是在你的思想中创造的。

积极的断言直接影响你的意识和潜意识。

为了有效地使用它们，请遵循以下三个基本方针：

1.将你的断言建立在对事实清楚的、理性的评估上，而不是一个幻想世界里。如果你是疲于应付满足你的基本需要的人，断言说："我能毫不费力地满足我的基本需要"要比说"我是一个百万富翁"更为有效，虽然真正的百万富翁通常能很好地利用积极的断言。

2.用现在时态来陈述自己的断言以便于你的思想知道你想要达到的目标正在发生。现在时态意味着："我已经"而不是在遥远的未来"我将要"。

3.在你的断言中使用积极的

will be effective while an affirmation saying: "I will not suffer anymore" will have the opposite effect. The mind registers the word "suffer" and neglects the "not anymore". It will do its best to create situations of suffering.

A very effective way to come up with[1] positive affirmations that are spots[2] on for you is to catch your negative thoughts and create their opposites.

If you think "I will never make it", the opposite could be "It's easy for me to achieve my goals" or "I see mistakes as a great opportunity to find out what works for me".

If you think "It's never enough", the opposites could be:

* Money is an unlimited reservoir of energy;

* I always have enough and will always have enough;

* I always have something to give;

* I give from my heart, and I know that it will return to me.

For the next three days, watch your thoughts. When you catch a negative one, write it down.

After three days, you will have noticed some favorites. You want to change those first.

词语。一个断言说："我很高兴和满意"，这样才会有效，而一个断言说："我不会再受苦了"会产生相反的效果。思想会将"吃苦"铭记于心，而忽略了"不会再"。思想就会尽最大努力创造痛苦的形势。

提出积极的断言来克服你性格上缺陷的一个好方法就是要捕抓到你的消极思想，创造它们的对立面。

如果你认为"永远完成不了它"，相反的就应该是"我很容易就能达到我的目标"或"我将错误看做是找到对我有利的事物的机会"。

如果你想"这永远是不够的"，相反的可以是：

* 金钱是无限的能量宝库；

* 我总是有足够的东西，将来也会永远足够；

* 我一直有东西用于给予；

* 我从心底给予，而且我知道我会有回报。

在未来的三天里，观察你的想法。当你发现消极的想法，就写下来。

三天后，你会注意到你的一些偏好。你首先要改变它们。

---

1 **come up with**: 找到，提出
2 **spot** /spɒt/ *n.* （性格上的）缺陷

含英咀华

在本文中作者首先告诉大家成功者和失败者的区别往往是由对自己心理暗示上的不同所造成的，然后作者给出建议：建立积极的心理暗示。文章的立意虽然有些老套，但整个文章结构清晰，语言流畅规范，读者不仅可以从文章中学到获取成功的法则，还可以学到地道的英文写作模式和用词技巧。

Muriel James & Dorothy Jongeward

穆理尔·詹姆斯&多萝西·琼基瓦德

穆理尔·詹姆斯和多萝西·琼基瓦德，两人同为美国著名的人力潜能开发专家和心理学作家，合作出版了多部心理学和励志学图书，本文选自他们的著作《生而为赢》(*Born to Win, 1988*)。

Born to Win

Each human being is born as something new, something that never exited before. Each is born with their capacity to win at life. Each person has a unique way of seeing, hearing, touching, tasting and thinking. Each has his or her own unique potentials — capabilities and limitations. Each can be significant, thinking, aware, and creative being — a productive person, a winner.

The word "winner" and "loser" have many meanings. When we refer to a person as a winner, we do not mean one who makes someone else lose. To us, a winner is one who responds authentically[1] by being credible, trustworthy, responsive, and genuine, both as an individual and as a member of a society.

Winners do not dedicate their lives to a concept of what they imagine they should be; rather, they are themselves and as such do not use their energy putting on a performance, maintaining pretence and manipulating others. They are aware that there is a difference between being loving and acting loving, between being stupid and acting stupid, between being knowledgeable and acting knowledgeable. Winners do not need to hide behind a mask.

Winners are not afraid to do their own thinking and to use their own knowledge. They can separate facts from opinions and don't pretend to have all the facts from opinions and don't pretend to have all the

生而为赢

人皆生而为新，为前所未有之存在。人皆生而能赢。人皆有其特立独行之方式去审视、聆听、触摸、品味及思考。人皆具备独特潜质——能力和局限。人皆能举足轻重，思虑明达，洞察秋毫，富有创意，成就功业。

"成者"与"败者"这两个词的含义颇多。谈及成者时我们并非指令他人失意之人。对我们而言，成者必为人守信，值得信赖，有求必应，态度诚恳，或为个人，或为社会的一员。

成者行事并不拘泥于某种信条，而是本色行事，所以并不把精力用来表演、伪装或操控他人。他们明白爱与装假爱，愚蠢与装傻，博学与卖弄之间迥然有别。成者无须藏于面具之后。

成者敢于利用所学，独立思考。他们能够区分事实与观点，且并不佯装通晓所有事实和答案。他们倾听、权衡

---

1 authentically /ɔːˈθentɪkli/ *adv.* 确实地

answers. They listen to others, evaluate what they say, but come to their own conclusions. Although winners can admire and respect other people, they are not totally defined, demolished[1], bound, or awed by them.

Winners do not play "helpless", nor do they play the blaming game. Instead, they assume responsibility for their own lives. They don't give others a false authority over them. Winners are their own bosses and know it.

A winner's timing is right. Winners respond appropriately to the situation. Their responses are related to the message sent and preserve the significance, worth, well-being, and dignity of the people involved. Winners know that for everything there is a season and for every activity a time.

Although winners can freely enjoy themselves, they can also postpone enjoyment; can discipline themselves in the present to enhance their enjoyment in the future. Winners are not afraid to go after what he wants, but they do so in proper ways. Winners do not get their security by controlling others. They do not set themselves up to lose.

A winner cares about the world and its peoples. A winner is not isolated from the general problems of society, but is concerned, compassionate, and committed to improving the quality of life. Even in the face of national and international adversity[2], a winner's self-image is not one of a powerless individual. A winner works to make the world a better place.

他人的意见，但能得出自己的结论。尽管他们尊重、敬佩他人，但并不为他人所局限、推翻、束缚，也不对他人敬若神明。

成者既不佯装"无助"，亦不抱怨他人。相反，他们总是独担人生责任。他们不以权威姿态凌驾于他人之上。他们主宰自己，而且深知这一点。

成者善于审时度势、随机应变。他们对所接受的信息做出回应，维护当事人的利益、康乐和尊严。成者深知成一事要看好时节，行一事要把握时机。

尽管成者可以自由享乐，但他更知如何推迟享乐，适时自律，以期将来乐趣更盛。成者并不忌惮追求所想，但取之有道，也并不靠控制他人来获取安然之感。他们总是使自己立于不败。

成者心忧天下，并不孤立于尘世弊病之外，而是置身事内，满腔热情，致力于改善民生。即使面对国家、世界之危亡，成者亦非无力回天之个体。他总是努力令世界更好。

---

1 demolish /dɪˈmɒlɪʃ/　v.　毁坏，破坏
2 adversity /ədˈvɜːsəti/　n.　不幸，灾难

含英咀华

文章首先点明主题，人生来就具备了所有使他能在生活中取得胜利的一切。然后以散文诗一般的语言从不同的角度对"成功者"下定义：成功者应不拘一格，应学以致用，不应自怨自艾，应审时度势，随机应变，既要自得其乐，又要心忧天下。全文诠释明确，措辞得当，说理通畅，议论充分，结构严谨。开头和结尾简洁明了，前后照应，紧扣文题；中心论点的提出，独立成段，干脆利落，短促有力。

Joseph Epstein
约瑟夫·艾本斯坦

约瑟夫·艾本斯坦(1937~)，美国散文作家、西北大学文学教授、《美国学者》(The American Scholar)杂志资深编辑、文化批评家，著述甚丰。作品有：散文集《熟悉的领域——美国生活观察》(Familiar Territory: Observations on American Life, 1979)、《似是而非的偏见——美国文学随笔》(Plausible Prejudices: Essays on American Writing, 1985)；短篇小说集《高尔丁的男孩们》(The Goldin Boys: Stories, 1991)、《惊人的小犹太佬》(Fabulous Small Jews, 2003)等。他的散文、书评常见于各大报纸和文学杂志，他的随笔继承了法国蒙田 (Michel de Montaigne)、英国兰姆 (Charles Lamb) 等的风格。

Ambition

It is not difficult to imagine a world short of ambition. It would probably be a kinder world: without demands, without abrasions, without disappointments. People would have time for reflection. Such work as they did would not be for themselves but for the collectivity[1]. Competition would never enter in, conflict would be eliminated[2], tension become a thing of the past. The stress of creation would be at an end. Art would no longer be troubling, but purely celebratory in its functions. Longevity[3] would be increased, for fewer people would die of heart attack or stroke[4] caused by tumultuous[5] endeavor[6]. Anxiety would be extinct. Time would stretch on and on, with ambition long departed from the human heart.

Ah, how unrelieved boring life would be!

There is a strong view that holds that success is a myth, and ambition therefore a sham[7]. Does this mean that success does not really exist? That achievement is at bottom empty? That the efforts of men and women are of no significance alongside the force of

抱负

不难想象一个缺乏抱负的世界将会怎样。或许，这将是一个更为友善的世界：没有渴求，没有纷争，没有失望。人们开始有时间进行反思。他们所从事的工作将不是为了他们自己，而是为了整个集体。竞争不再存在，冲突将被消除，人们的紧张关系将成为过往。创造的重压将得以终结。艺术不再惹人费神，其功能将只是纯粹的庆祝。人的寿命将会更长，因为由激烈拼争引起的心脏病和中风所导致的死亡将越来越少。焦虑将会消失。随着抱负远离人心，时间也将无限延伸。

啊，长此以往人生将多么乏味无聊！

有一种强势的观点认为，成功是一种神话，因此抱负亦属虚幻。这是不是意味着成功并不真正存在呢？成就本身就是一场空吗？与诸多运动和事件的力量

---

1 collectivity /kə,lek'tɪvəti/　n.　集体
2 eliminate /ɪ'lɪmɪneɪt/　v.　除去，排除，剔除
3 longevity /lɒn'dʒevəti/　n.　长寿
4 stroke /strəʊk/　n.　中风
5 tumultuous /tju:'mʌltʃuəs/　adj.　乱哄哄的，喧哗的
6 endeavor /ɪn'devə(r)/　n.　努力，尽力
7 sham /ʃæm/　n.　假货，赝品，骗子

movements and events? Now not all success, obviously, is worth esteeming[1], nor all ambition worth cultivating. Which are and which are not is something one soon enough learns on one's own. But even the most cynical secretly admit that success exists; that achievement counts for a great deal; and that the true myth is that the actions of men and women are useless. To believe otherwise is to take on a point of view that is likely to be deranging. It is, in its implications, to remove all motives for competence, interest in attainment, and regard for posterity.

We do not choose to be born. We do not choose our parents. We do not choose our historical epoch[2], the country of our birth, or the immediate circumstances of our upbringing[3]. We do not, most of us, choose to die; nor do we choose the time or conditions of our death. But within all this realm of choicelessness, we do choose how we shall live: courageously or in cowardice[4], honorably or dishonorably, with purpose or in drift. We decide what is important and what is trivial[5] in life. We decide that what makes us significant is either what we do or what we refuse to do. But no matter how indifferent the universe may be to our choices and decisions, these choices and decisions are ours to make.

1 esteem /ɪˈstiːm/　v.　尊敬，尊重
2 epoch /ˈiːpɒk/　n.　（新）纪元，（新）时代
3 upbringing /ˈʌpbrɪŋɪŋ/　n.　教养
4 cowardice /ˈkaʊədɪs/　n.　懦弱
5 trivial /ˈtrɪvɪəl/　adj.　琐碎的，不重要的

相比，男男女女的努力显得微不足道？显然，并非所有的成功都值得景仰，也并非所有的抱负都值得培养。对值得和不值得的选择，一个人自己很快就能学会。但即使是最为愤世嫉俗的人暗地里也会承认，成功确实存在，成功有着非常重大的意义，而把人们的所作所为说成是徒劳无功才是真正的无稽之谈。认为成功不存在的观点很可能造成混乱。这种观点的实质是否定所有提高能力的动机，否定求取成就的兴趣和对子孙后代的关注。

我们无法选择出生，无法选择父母，无法选择出生的时代与国家或是成长的环境背景。我们大多数人都无法选择死亡，也无法选择死亡的时间或条件。但是在这些无法选择之中，我们的确可以选择自己的生活方式：是勇敢无畏还是胆小怯懦，是光明磊落还是厚颜无耻，是雄心壮志还是随波逐流。我们决定生活中哪些至关重要，哪些微不足道。我们通过有所为而又有所不为显示出自己的重要性。但是不论世界对我们所做的选择和决定有多么漠不关心，这些选择和决定终究是我们自己做出的。我们决定，我们选择。而当我们

We decide. We choose. And as we decide and choose, so are our lives formed. In the end, forming our own destiny is what ambition is about.

决定和选择时，我们的生活便得以形成。最终，抱负的意义就在于创造我们自己的命运。

含英咀华

　　本文文笔清新脱俗，妙语连珠，读来让人击节。无论是其语言，还是其观点都让人觉得是一种巨大的精神享受，尤其是在当今文人自甘堕落的时代，这篇文章更让人有一种遗世独立之感。其中，最能引起共鸣的就是最后一个段落，"我们无法选择出生，无法选择父母，无法选择出生的时代与国家或是成长的环境背景。我们大多数人都无法选择死亡，也无法选择死亡的时间或条件。但是在这些无法选择之中，我们的确可以选择自己的生活方式：是勇敢无畏还是胆小怯懦，是光明磊落还是厚颜无耻，是雄心壮志还是随波逐流。"

Andrew Carnegie
安德鲁·卡耐基

安德鲁·卡耐基(1835~1919)，出生于苏格兰，十二岁时随家人移居到美国，他是白手起家的美国钢铁大王、哲学家和慈善家，受到了世人的广泛瞩目。他做过多种工作，也投资过多种事业，为英美的许多公共机关捐献了数以百万计的巨款。人们公认卡耐基是世界首富，在美国任何一个城市中，都有以他的名字命名的图书馆。他的主要著作有：《财富的福音》(The Gospel of Wealth, 1889)、《卡耐基自传》(Autobiography of Andrew Carnegie, 1920)等。

The Road to Success

It is well that young men should begin at the beginning and occupy the most subordinate[1] positions. Many of the leading businessmen of Pittsburgh[2] had a serious responsibility thrust[3] upon them at the very threshold[4] of their career. They were introduced to the broom, and spent the first hours of their business lives sweeping out the office. I notice we have janitors[5] and janitresses[6] now in offices, and our young men unfortunately miss that salutary[7] branch of business education. But if by chance the professional sweeper is absent any morning, the boy who has the genius of the future partner in him will not hesitate to try his hand at the broom. It does not hurt the newest comer to sweep out the office if necessary. I was one of those sweepers myself.

Assuming that you have all obtained employment and are fairly started, my advice to you is "aim high". I would not give a fig[8] for the young man who does not already see himself the partner or the head of an

成功之道

年轻人应该从头学起，担当最基层的职务，这是件好事。匹兹堡有很多商业巨头，在他们创业之初都肩负过"重任"：他们与扫帚相伴，以打扫办公室的方式度过了他们商业生涯中最初的时光。我注意到现在的办公室里雇用了工友，这使我们的年轻人很可惜地错过了企业教育中这个有益的环节。但是，假如碰巧哪天上午专职扫地的工友没有来，某个具有未来合伙人气质的年轻人会毫不犹豫地拿起扫帚扫地。如果有必要，新来的员工打扫办公室以外的地方也无妨，不会因此而有什么损失。我就这么做过。

假如你已经被录用，还有一个良好的开端，我对你的建议是："要胸怀大志"。一个年轻人，如果不把自己看成公司未来的老板或是合伙人，

---

1 **subordinate** /səˈbɔːdɪnət/ *adj.* 下级的，次要的，附属的
2 **Pittsburgh** *n.* 匹兹堡（美国宾夕法尼亚州西南部城市，是美国的钢铁工业中心）
3 **thrust** /θrʌst/ *v.* 逼迫，将……强加于
4 **threshold** /ˈθreʃhəuld/ *n.* 入口，开端
5 **janitor** /ˈdʒænɪtə(r)/ *n.* 守卫，门警，管理人，工友
6 **janitress** /ˈdʒænɪtris/ *n.* 女性守卫，女性门警
7 **salutary** /ˈsæljətri/ *adj.* 有益的，有用的，有益健康的
8 **fig** /fɪg/ *n.* 无价值的东西；[植]无花果。**give a fig (for sb./sth.)** 对……丝毫不在乎

important firm. Do not rest content for a moment in your thoughts as head clerk, or foreman[1], or general manager in any concern, no matter how extensive. Say to yourself, "My place is at the top." Be king in your dreams.

And here is the prime condition of success, the great secret: concentrate your energy, thought, and capital exclusively[2] upon the business in which you are engaged. Having begun in one line, resolve to fight it out on that line, to lead in it, adopt every improvement, have the best machinery, and know the most about it.

The concerns which fail are those which have scattered[3] their capital, which means that they have scattered their brains also. They have investments in this, or that, or the other, here, there, and everywhere. "Don't put all your eggs in one basket." is all wrong. I tell you to "put all your eggs in one basket, and then watch that basket." Look round you and take notice, men who do that not often fail. It is easy to watch and carry the one basket. It is trying to carry too many baskets that breaks most eggs in this country. He who carries three baskets must put one on his head, which is apt to tumble[4] and trip him up[5].

1 foreman /ˈfɔːmən/ n. 领班，工头，陪审长
2 exclusively /ɪkˈskluːsɪvli/ adv. 排他地（独占地，专门地，仅仅，只）
3 scatter /ˈskætə(r)/ v. 散开，散布，散播
4 tumble /ˈtʌmbl/ v. 翻倒，摔倒，倒塌
5 trip up （使）犯错误，把……绊倒。例如:Harry was running well until he tripped up and fell, losing the race.（哈利本来一直跑得很好，可后来绊了一跤，输了比赛。）

那我会对他不屑一顾。不管公司的规模有多大，永远不要满足于只担任一个首席员工，领班或者总经理。要告诉自己："我的地位是在顶端！" 要做就做你梦想中的国王！

成功的首要条件和最大秘诀就是：把你所有的精力、思想和资本都集中在你正从事的事业上。一旦开始从事某种职业，就要下定决心在那一领域闯出一片天地来，做这一行的领导人物，采纳每一个改进措施，采用最先进的设备，通晓所有相关知识。

一些公司的失败就在于他们分散了资金，因为这就意味着分散了他们的精力。他们投资这个，投资那个或者其他项目；在这里那里都投资，方方面面都投资。"不要把所有的鸡蛋都放在一个篮子里"的说法大错特错。我告诉你们，要"把所有的鸡蛋都放在一个篮子里，然后要照顾好这个篮子。"看看你周围的人，你会注意到：这么做的人其实很少失败。管好并提好一个篮子并不太难。在我们的国家，想要多提篮子的人打碎的鸡蛋最多。一个人如果要提三个篮子的话，就必须把一个顶在头

锲而不舍 金石可镂

One fault of the American businessman is lack of concentration.

To summarize what I have said: aim for the highest; never enter a bar room; do not touch liquor, or if at all only at meals; never speculate[1]; never indorse[2] beyond your surplus[3] cash fund; make the firm's interest yours; break orders always to save owners; concentrate; put all your eggs in one basket, and watch that basket; expenditure always within revenue; lastly, be not impatient, for as Emerson says, "no one can cheat you out of ultimate success but yourselves."

上，而这个篮子很可能掉下来，把他自己绊倒。美国企业家就缺少这种集中精神。

把我的话归纳一下：要立志成为最好的；不要涉足酒吧；不要喝酒，如不能避免也只在用餐时喝；千万不要投机；不要寅吃卯粮；要把公司的利益当做自己的利益；取消订货的目的永远在于挽救货主；集中精力；要把所有的鸡蛋都放在一个篮子里，并且照看好这个篮子；要量入为出；最后，不要失去耐心，因为爱默生说过，"除了你自己，没有人能够将最终的成功从你手中骗走。"

1 speculate /ˈspekjuleɪt/　v.　深思，推测，投机
2 indorse /ɪnˈdɔːs/　v.　(=endorse) 签名于票据等的背面，认可
3 surplus /ˈsɜːpləs/　n.　过剩，剩余物，盈余，顺差

含英咀华

卡耐基的话并不是像一般意义上的说教一样，他的话是从实践中总结出来的。从这篇文章中我们就能体会出，他告诉我们成功并没有什么玄妙的捷径，无非是从最低的职位做起，踏踏实实地干；要有雄心壮志；要集中精力放在一项事业上。最后，作者进行了更细节化的总结。总之，奋斗就会有艰辛，为了更好的明天拼命努力终究会获取胜利的果实。

Florence Scovel Shinn
弗洛伦斯·斯科维尔·希恩

弗洛伦斯·斯科威尔·希恩 (1871—1940)，艺术家、作家。在20世纪早期，她曾经在纽约任教，教形而上学的课程。同时，她也是一位善于写励志书籍的女作家。她书里的文章通常都很短，内容常常涉及的是怎样赢取健康、怎样获得成功以及如何保持乐观的心态等。她会用发生在自己身上的例子来证实自己的观点。主要作品有《生命中的游戏及怎样赢取它们》(The Game of Life and how to Play it, 1925)、《言语的力量》(Your Word is Your Wand, 1928)、《通往成功的神秘之门》(The Secret Door to Success, 1940) 等等。

The Fork in the Road

Every day there is a necessity of choice (a fork in the road). "Shall I do this? Or shall I do that? Shall I go, or shall stay?" Many people do not know what to do. They rush about letting other people make decisions for them, then regret having taken their advice.

There are others who carefully reason things out[1]. They weigh and measure the situation like dealing in groceries, and are surprised when they fail to obtain their goal.

There are still other people who follow the magic path of intuition and find themselves in their Promised Land in the twinkling of an eye.

Intuition is a spiritual faculty[2] high above the reasoning mind, but on the path is all that you desire or require. So choose ye this day to follow the magic path of intuition.

In most people it is a faculty which has remained dormant[3]. So we say, "Awake though that sleeps. Wake up to your leads and hunches[4]!"

Now it is necessary for you to make a decision, you face a fork in the road. Ask for

面对人生的岔路口

我们每天都要面临不同的选择。"是该这样，还是该那样？我是要走还是要留？"许多人都很茫然，于是他们跑去让别人替他们拿主意，然而又因为听了他人的意见而后悔。

当然，也会有人为自己的前途仔细思量。他们就像经营杂货店一样经营着自己的未来，还会惊讶于自己没有实现自己的目标。

还有一些人会跟着感觉走，转眼之间就到了他们梦想中的天堂。

直觉是一种高于理性思想的本能，然而，只有当你有着强烈欲望或者迫切需要的时候，这种本能才会显现出来。所以，相信自己的直觉，跟着感觉走吧！

但大多数人的这种本能还未被唤醒。所以，我们要说，"醒来吧！唤醒沉睡的直觉

---

1 reason out 推论出。例如 The police reasoned out that if the criminal had left by the midday train, it would be easy to pick him up at the terminus. （警察部门推断，如果那个罪犯是乘中午列车离开的，那就容易在终点站把他捉住。）
2 faculty /ˈfæklti/ n. 才能，能力
3 dormant /ˈdɔːmənt/ adj. 睡眠状态的，静止的
4 hunch /hʌntʃ/ n. 预感

a definite unmistakable lead, and you will receive it.

So we find we have success though being strong and very courageous in following spiritual law.

A well-known man, who has become a great power in the financial world, said to a friend, "I always follow intuition and luck incarnates[1]."

Inspiration[2] is the most important thing in life. I find the right word will start divine[3] activity operating in their affairs.

In every act prompted by fear lies the germ[4] of its own defeat.

吧，唤醒心中的巨人吧！"

现在，你正面临着一个十字路口，到你做决定的时候了。看看你的直觉会给你一个怎样的确定答案，然后，勇敢尝试一下！

我们会发现，成功的路上有了直觉为伴，我们变得愈加强大，愈加勇敢。

一位金融界的成功人士对他的朋友说："我从来都是跟着感觉走的，而幸运也总是降临到我身上！"

灵感是人的一生中最重要的一种能量。有了灵感，人们在工作时就会如鱼得水，应变自如。

任一恐惧行为都会为我们的失败埋下祸根。

---

1 incarnate /'ɪnkɑːneɪt/ v. 使实体化；使具体化；体现
2 inspiration /ˌɪnspə'reɪʃn/ n. 灵感
3 divine /dɪ'vaɪn/ adj. 神的，神圣的
4 germ /dʒɜːm/ n. 种子；幼芽；胚芽

含英咀华

希恩对直觉有着自己的见解，她希望告诉大家，相信直觉，因为只有这样不畏首畏尾，你才能取得成功。"三思而后行"似乎不适合青年人，因为机会转瞬即逝，在人生的十字路口上，不要过多的犹豫、徘徊，因为我们年轻，即使错了，我们也有资本重新来过。

及时当勉励
岁月不待人

Youth
青春

Man's Youth
人的青春

On the Feeling of Immortality in Youth
有感于青春常在

Samuel Ullman

塞缪尔·厄尔曼

塞缪尔·厄尔曼（1840~1924），生于德国，童年时移居美国。参加过南北战争，后来定居于亚拉巴马州的伯明翰市。他是一位五金制品商，热心公益六十多年。

Youth

青春

Youth is not a time of life; it is a state of mind; it is not a matter of rosy cheeks, red lips and supple[1] knees; it is a matter of the will, a quality of the imagination, a vigor of the emotions; it is the freshness of the deep springs of life.

Youth means a temperamental[2] predominance[3] of courage over timidity of the appetite, for adventure over the love of ease. This often exists in a man of sixty more than a body of twenty. Nobody grows old merely by a number of years. We grow old by deserting our ideals.

Years may wrinkle[4] the skin, but to give up enthusiasm wrinkles the soul. Worry, fear and self-distrust bow the heart and turn the spirit back to dust.

Whether sixty or sixteen, there is in every human being's heart the lure[5] of wonder, the unfailing child-like appetite of what's next, and the joy of the game of living. In the center of your heart and my heart there is a wireless station; so long as it receives messages of beauty, hope, cheer, courage and power from

青春不是年华，而是心境；青春不在于桃面朱唇之艳，灵活矫健之躯，而在于志士之气，遐想之境，激情之盛；青春有如生命的源泉，涓涌不息。

青春气贯长虹，勇锐盖过怯懦，进取压倒苟安。如此锐气，弱冠后生有之，耳顺之年，则亦多见。年岁有加，未必已垂老；理想若失，则已堕暮年。

岁月流逝，衰老仅及肌肤；抛却热忱，颓废必至灵魂。忧虑、惶恐、丧失自信定使心灵扭曲，意气如灰。

无论年届花甲抑或年方二八，世人心中皆有生命之欢乐，奇迹之诱惑，未泯童心久盛不衰。人人心中仿佛都有一电台，只要接收美丽、希望、欢乐、勇气和力量的信号，定能青春永驻，风华长存。

1 supple /'sʌpl/ *adj.* 柔软的，顺从的
2 temperamental /ˌtemprə'mentl/ *adj.* 性情的，喜怒无常的
3 predominance /prɪ'dɒmɪnəns/ *n.* 卓越，优势，控制
4 wrinkle /'rɪŋkl/ *v.* 使皱，起皱
5 lure /ljʊə(r)/ *n.* 饵，诱惑

men and from the infinite[1], so long are you young.

When the aerials[2] are down, and your spirit is covered with snows of cynicism[3] and the ice of pessimism, then you are grown old, even at twenty, but as long as your aerials are up, to catch the waves of optimism, there is hope you may die young at eighty.

若心中的电台的天线倒下，锐气将如同被冰雪覆盖一般，玩世不恭、自暴自弃则油然而生，即使年仅二十，实已垂垂老矣！但若能竖起天线，捕捉乐观的信号，八十高龄告别尘寰时，仍能感觉年轻依旧。

1 infinite /ˈɪnfɪnət/　*n.*　无限
2 aerial /ˈeəriəl/　*n.*　天线
3 cynicism /ˈsɪnɪsɪzəm/　*n.*　玩世不恭，愤世嫉俗

含英咀华

　　本文激励那些心灵需要安慰的人，给忧郁、消沉的人以生命的勇气和力量，让人们怀着信心去生活。著名的格拉斯·麦克阿瑟将军经常引用厄尔曼的《青春》一文，并且在整个太平洋战争期间，将其镶入镜框作为座右铭。据传，日本人就是从他在东京的占领军总部得到它的，所以至今仍有许多日本名流将其珍藏于随身携带的钱夹之中。一位资深的日本问题观察家说过："在日本实业界，凡是有所成就的人，无不知晓并且应用过这篇文章(Anyone worth his salt in Japanese business knows and uses this essay.)。"富士产经通讯集团的副总裁石田达郎曾把它比喻为"大力水手吃的菠菜"(Popeye's spinach)。

Thomas Wolfe
托马斯·沃尔夫

托马斯·沃尔夫（1900~1938）是三十年代活跃在美国文坛的著名小说家。他以情感旋律作为小说的内在结构，继承了以惠特曼、爱默生和马克·吐温为代表的一代美国文化名流所创立的以边疆生活为核心的、贴近生活、朴实奔放的文学传统，文风豪放，抒情色彩浓郁。长期以来评论界对他的小说创作形式毁誉参半，但他个性化的抒情性表现风格以及他融入小说语言中感官色彩浓郁的直观表现方式使他的作品独具特色、风格迥异。他的小说因此染上了浓重的史诗性色彩，赢得了广大读者的青睐。他的主要作品有《天使，望故乡》(Look Homeward, Angel, 1929)、《时间与河流》(Of Time and the River, 1935)、《蛛网与岩石》(The Web and the Rock, 1939)、《有家归不得》(You Can't Go Home Again, 1940) 等等。

Man's Youth

Man's youth is a wonderful thing: it is so full of anguish[1] and of magic and he never comes to know it as it is, until it has gone from him forever. It is the thing he cannot bear to lose, it is the thing whose passing he watches with infinite sorrow and regret, it is the thing whose loss he must lament[2] forever, it is the thing whose loss he really welcomes with a sad and secret joy, the thing he would never willingly relive again, could it be restored to him by any magic.

Why is this? The reason is that the strange and bitter miracle of life is nowhere else so evident as in our youth. And what is the essence of that strange and bitter miracle of life which we feel so poignantly[3], so unutterably[4], with such a bitter pain and joy, when we are young? It is this: that being rich, we are so poor; that being mighty, we can yet have nothing; that seeing, breathing, smelling, tasting all around us the impossible wealth and glory of this earth, feeling with an intolerable certitude[5] that the whole structure of the enchanted life — the most fortunate, wealthy, good, and happy life that any man has ever known — is ours — is ours at once, immediately and forever, the moment

人的青春

青春年少精彩奇妙，既充满痛楚，又魅力无穷。少时不知青春为何物，至其永逝，方始恍然痛惜。青春流逝让人万般不舍，目睹其渐行渐远，不免伤怀难遣，日夜追悔；老之将至固然叫人唏嘘不已，但青春不再又确实令人暗自悲喜交加；而纵有奇迹唤春归来，却任谁也不愿重度那青涩岁月。

这该做何解呢？这是因为，人生的奇幻乖舛在年少时光最显淋漓酣畅。此时，个中滋味是如此深刻痛切，如此无以名状，如此苦乐交织。然而，当我们年轻时，这奇妙苦涩的人生到底是什么呢？其本质就是：年轻时，虽富足无缺，实一贫如洗；虽强壮有力，却一无所有。这时，原以为世间绝无的荣华富贵，却时刻耳闻目睹，因而涌现无比的自信——人世极致的幸福、美好、财富、快乐，肯定非我们莫属，不但唾手可得，而且

1 anguish /ˈæŋgwɪʃ/   *n.*   苦闷，痛苦
2 lament /ləˈment/   *v.*   哀悼，悔恨，悲叹
3 poignantly /ˈpɔɪnjəntli/   *adv.*   痛切地，辛辣地
4 unutterably /ʌnˈʌtərəbli/   *adv.*   非语言所能表达地（坏透地）
5 certitude /ˈsɜːtɪtjuːd/   *n.*   确实，确信

that we choose to take a step, or stretch a hand, or say a word — we yet know that we can really keep, hold, take, and possess forever — nothing. All passes; nothing lasts: the moment that we put our hand upon it, it melts away like smoke, is gone forever, and the snake is eating at our heart again; we see then what we are and what our lives must come to.

A young is so strong, so mad, so certain, and so lost. He has everything and he is able to use nothing. He hurls the great shoulder of his strength forever against phantasmal[1] barriers, he is a wave whose power explodes in lost mid-oceans under timeless skies, he reaches out to grip a fume[2] of painted smoke; he wants all, feels the thirst and power for everything, and finally gets nothing. In the end, he is destroyed by his own strength, devoured by his own hunger, improvised by his own wealth. Thoughtless of money or the accumulation of material possessions, he is none the less defeated in the end by his own greed — a greed that makes the avarice[3] of King Midas[4] seem paltry by comparison.

And that is the reason why, when youth is gone, every man will look back upon that period of his life with infinite sorrow and regret. It is the bitter sorrow and regret of a man who knows that once he had a great talent and wasted it, of a man who knows that once he had a great

1 phantasmal /fænˈtæzəml/ adj. 幻影的，幽灵一样的
2 fume /fjuːm/ n. 臭气，烟
3 avarice /ˈævərɪs/ n. 贪财，贪婪
4 King Midas: 迈达斯国王，古希腊神话中的一个贪财者，拥有"点金术"，可使其财富增加，却失去许多远比黄金更宝贵的东西

永保不失。然而，当真举步向前、伸手抓拿、张口发话时，才赫然发觉，我们所能取得、可以拥有的，竟空无一物。一切飘然而过，无一永恒长存，只要伸手触及，立刻烟消云散，永不复返。于是心中又有如蛇噬，因为此时此刻，我们已看清自己这点能耐，明白此生之无奈。

年轻人强健、疯狂、自信，但同样也会很失落。他具有一切，却无以致用，他永远地靠着强健的体魄，对着心中的障碍知难而上；他是一股热浪，在无限的苍穹下，在海洋中爆发自己的力量，他伸出手，去抓一缕着色的轻烟；他想拥有一切，渴求世间所有的东西，觉得自己有力量得到它们，而结果却徒劳无功。最后，被自己的力量毁灭，被自己的欲望吞噬，自己的财富让他变得一贫如洗。在钱财和物质财富积累方面没有规划，到了最后还是自己的贪婪打倒了自己——即便是迈达斯国王的欲望与其相比也显得无足轻重。

当青春已逝，每个人都会怀着无尽的悲哀和遗憾回首那段生活，其原因也在于此。曾经才智卓越，却一无所用；曾

treasure and got nothing from it, of a man who knows that he had strength enough for everything and never used it.

经殷实富足，却一无所有；曾经身强力壮，却一事无成。

及时当勉励　岁月不待人

含英咀华

本文是一篇慨叹青春的文章，作者的语言朴实，文字流畅，一方面体味着青春的美好，另一方面又惋惜着青春逝去的遗憾。读起来颇有点辛弃疾笔下那首《丑奴儿》的味道："少年不识愁滋味，爱上层楼。爱上层楼，为赋新词强说愁。而今识尽愁滋味，欲说还休。欲说还休，却道天凉好个秋。"文中以过来人的口吻告诫青年人不要浪费青春，不要待到青春消逝才追悔莫及。

William Hazlitt

托马威廉·赫兹里特

威廉·赫兹里特（1778～1830）是19世纪初英国著名的浪漫主义流派散文作家。他重感性和想象，张扬个性，反对权威和陈规陋习；主张多样和宽容，反对狭隘和专制；支持进步和革命，反对保守和停滞，是19世纪浪漫主义运动中的一位重要代表。散文，是赫兹里特一生中主要的文学成就。他的散文主要分为评论和随笔两大类。在他的随笔写作中，以《燕谈录》(Table-Talk, 1821～1822)、《直言集》(Liber Amoris, 1823) 影响最大。而《燕谈录》不仅是赫兹里特的代表作，也是一部为名家所推崇的名著。

及时当勉励 岁月不待人

On the Feeling of Immortality in Youth

有感于青春常在

No young man believes he shall ever die. It was a saying of my brother's, and a fine one. There is a feeling of Eternity[1] in youth, which makes us amend[2] for everything. To be young is to be as one of the Immortal[3] Gods. One half of time indeed is flown — the other half remains in store for us with all its countless treasures; for there is no line drawn, and we see no limit to our hopes and wishes. We make the coming age our own — The vast, the unbounded[4] prospect lies before us.

Death, old age, are words without a meaning, that pass by us like the idea air which we regard not. Others may have undergone, or may still be liable to them — we "bear a charmed life", which laughs to scorn all such sickly fancies. As in setting out on delightful journey, we strain our eager gaze forward — Bidding the lovely scenes at distance hail!

— and see no end to the landscape, new objects presenting themselves as we advance; so, in the commencement[5] of life, we set no bounds to

没有年轻人相信自己会死去。这是我哥哥的话，它真算得上一句妙语。青春有一种永生之感——它能弥补一切。拥有青春的人就好似一尊不朽的神灵。一半的生命已经流走，但蕴藏着无尽宝藏的另一半生命还有所保留，由于其不存在下限，因此，我们对它也就抱着无穷的希望和幻想。我们把未来的时代完全据为己有——无限辽阔的远景在我们面前展现。

死亡、老迈，不过是句空话，没有任何意义，我们听了，如同耳边风一样，并没有放在心上。这些事，别人也许经历过，或者可能正在经历，但是我们自己"在灵符护佑下度日"，对于诸如此类脆弱的念头，统统会轻蔑地一笑了之。像是刚刚走上愉快的旅程，极目远眺——向远方美好的景象欢呼！

——此时，我们会觉得好风景无边无际，如果往前走的话，还会有更多美不胜收的新鲜景致。在生活的开端，我

1 eternity /ɪˈtɜːnəti/ *n.* 永远，来世，不朽
2 amend /əˈmend/ *v.* 修正，改善，改良
3 immortal /ɪˈmɔːtl/ *adj.* 不朽的
4 unbounded /ʌnˈbaʊndɪd/ *adj.* 无限的
5 commencement /kəˈmensmənt/ *n.* 开始；毕业典礼

our inclinations, nor to the unrestricted opportunities of gratifying[1] them. We have as yet found no obstacle, no disposition to flag; and it seems that we can go on so forever. We look round in a new world, full of life, and motion, and ceaseless[2] progress; and feel in ourselves all the vigour and spirit to keep pace with it, and do not foresee from any present symptoms[3] how we shall be left behind in the natural course of things, decline into old age, and drop into the grave. It is the simplicity, and as it were abstractedness[4] of our feelings in youth, that (so to speak) identifies us with nature, and (our experience being slight and our passions strong) deludes[5] us into a belief of being immortal like it. Our short-lived connexion with existence we fondly flatter ourselves, is an indissoluble[6] and lasting union — a honeymoon that knows neither coldness, jar, nor separation. As infants smile and sleep, we are rocked in the cradle[7] of our wayward fancies, and lulled[8] into security by the roar of the universe around us — we quaff[9] the cup of life with eager haste without draining it, instead of which it only overflows the more — objects press around us, filling the mind with their magnitude and with the strong of desires that wait upon them, so that we have no room for the thoughts of death.

1 gratify /'ɡrætɪfaɪ/ v. 使高兴；使满意
2 ceaseless /'siːsləs/ adj. 不绝的，不停的
3 symptom /'sɪmptəm/ n 症状；征兆
4 abstractedness /æbˈstræktɪdnɪs/ n. 出神，发呆
5 delude /dɪˈluːd/ v. 迷惑，蛊惑
6 indissoluble /ˌɪndɪˈsɒljəbl/ adj. 不能溶解的，不能分解的；坚固的
7 cradle /'kreɪdl/ n. 摇篮；发祥地
8 lull /lʌl/ v. 平息，使……平静，哄
9 quaff /kwɒf/ v. 豪饮；开怀畅饮

们听任自己的志趣驰骋，放手给它们一切满足的机会。到目前为止，我们还没有碰上过什么障碍，也没有感觉到疲倦，因而觉得可以一直这样向前走下去，直到永远。我们看到四周一派新天地，生机盎然，变动不定，日新月异，我们觉得自己充满活力，精神高涨。而且，眼前也没有任何迹象可以表明，在大自然的发展过程中，我们自己也会落伍、衰老，进入坟墓。年轻人天性单纯，可以说是茫然无知，总是有青春常在之感，因而将自己跟大自然画上等号。并且，由于缺少经验，感情旺盛，总是以为自己也能像大自然一样永世长存。我们在世界上只是暂时栖身，却一厢情愿、痴心妄想地竟把它当做千古不变的结合，好像没有冷漠、争吵、离别的蜜月。像婴儿带着微笑入睡一样，我们躺在用自己天真的幻想所织成的摇篮里，让大千世界的万籁之声把我们催眠，我们高兴而急切地畅饮生命之杯，怎么也不会饮干，好像永远满得要溢出来一样：一切包罗万象纷至沓来，各种欲望随之而生，我们都腾不出时间去思考死亡。

及时当勉励　岁月不待人

含英咀华

在《有感于青春常在》这篇散文中，作者围绕一个永恒的话题"青春"讲述了自己的感受。青春常在吗？答案当然是否定的。可年轻人们却总认为死亡离自己十分遥远，青春就像杯中的美酒一般，"怎么也不会饮干，好像永远满得要溢出来一样"。千万不要让人生中最宝贵的青春就这样轻易地消逝，因为青春只有一次，因为青春一去不再复返。本文风格清新、优美，用词考究得当，富有感染力。

不经一番寒彻骨
怎得梅花扑鼻香

Henry Van Dyke

亨利·范·戴克

亨利·范·戴克（1852~1933），美国短篇小说家、著名的诗人和散文家。他毕业于普林斯顿大学神学院，后来成为一位卓越的长老会牧师，其间曾担任普林斯顿大学英国文学教授。威尔逊总统曾派他出任驻荷兰及卢森堡大使。第一次世界大战时他曾任美国海军军中牧师。他的著作包括散文、诗集及灵修书籍等。作品寓情于理，娓娓道来，让人在潜移默化中受到感染。

A Handful of Clay[1]

There was a handful of clay in the bank of a river. It was only common clay, coarse and heavy; but it had high thoughts of its own value, and wonderful dreams of the great place which it was to fill in the world when the time came for its virtues to be discovered.

Overhead, in the spring sunshine, the trees whispered together of the glory which descended upon them when the delicate blossoms and leaves began to expand, and the forest glowed[2] with fair, clear colors, as if the dust of thousands of rubies[3] and emeralds[4] were hanging, in soft clouds, above the earth.

The flowers, surprised with the joy of beauty, bent their heads to one another, as the wind caressed them, and said: "Sisters, how lovely you have become. You make the day bright."

The river, glad of new strength and rejoicing in the unison of all its waters, murmured to the shores in music, telling of its release from icy fetters, its swift flight from the snow-clad mountains, and the mighty work to which it was hurrying — the wheels of many mills to be turned, and great ships to be floated to the sea.

1　clay /kleɪ/　*n.*　黏土；陶土
2　glow /gləʊ/　*v.*　发出微弱而稳定的光
3　ruby /'ruːbi/　*n.*　红宝石，深红色
4　emerald /'emərəld/　*n.*　翡翠；绿宝石

一撮黏土

从前在一条河边有这么一撮黏土。说来也不过是普通的黏土，质地粗拙；但他对自己的价值却抱有很高的看法，对它在世界上所可能占有的地位具有奇妙的梦想，认为一旦时运到来，自己的优点终将为人发现。

春天，树木在阳光下窃窃私语，谈论着他们在花开叶绿时得到的荣誉。森林里呈现出美丽而清晰的色彩，好像在柔软的白云中，在大地的上空，悬挂着数千粒红宝石和绿宝石似的。

花儿因美貌的欢乐而受宠若惊，它们互相点着头，风抚着花儿说："姐妹们，你们长得多么媚人啊！你们使白天显得更欢快。"

河水也因为增添了新的力量而感到高兴，它沉浸在水流重聚的欢乐之中，不断以美好的音调向河岸喃喃絮语，叙述着自己是怎么挣脱冰雪的束缚，怎么从积雪覆盖的群山奔腾来到这里，以及它匆忙前往担负的重大工作 —— 无数水车的轮子等待着它去推动，巨大的船只等待着它去送往海上。

Waiting blindly in its bed, the clay comforted itself with lofty hopes. "My time will come," it said. "I was not made to be hidden forever. Glory and beauty and honor are coming to me in due season."

One day the clay felt itself taken from the place where it had waited so long. A flat blade of iron passed beneath it, and lifted it, and tossed[1] it into a cart with other lumps of clay, and it was carried far away, as it seemed, over a rough and stony road. But it was not afraid, nor discouraged, for it said to itself: "This is necessary. The path to glory is always rugged. Now I am on my way to play a great part in the world."

But the hard journey was nothing compared with the tribulation[2] and distress[3] that came after it. The clay was put into a trough and mixed and beaten and stirred and trampled[4]. It seemed almost unbearable. But there was consolation[5] in the thought that something very fine and noble was certainly coming out of all this trouble. The clay felt sure that, if it could only wait long enough, a wonderful reward was in store for it.

Then it was put upon a swiftly turning wheel, and whirled around until it seemed as if it must fly into a thousand pieces. A strange power pressed it and molded it, as it revolved, and through all the dizziness[6] and pain it felt that it was taking a

1 toss /tɒs/　v.　投掷；摇荡；辗转
2 tribulation /ˌtrɪbjuˈleɪʃn/　n.　苦难，灾难
3 distress /dɪˈstres/　n.　苦恼，贫困
4 trample /ˈtræmpl/　v.　践踏
5 consolation /ˌkɒnsəˈleɪʃn/　n.　安慰
6 dizziness /ˈdɪzɪnɪs/　n.　头昏眼花

黏土懵懵懂懂地待在河床，不断用种种远大理想来安慰自己。"我的时运终将到来，"它说，"我是不会长久被埋没的。世间的种种光彩、荣耀，在适当的时候，会降临到我的头上。"

一天，黏土发现它自己挪了位置，不在原来长期苦守的地方了。一铲下去，它被挖了起来，然后和别的泥土一起被装到一辆车上，沿着一条看来很不平坦的石子路，被运到遥远的地方去。但它并不害怕，也不气馁，而只是心里在想："这完全是必要的。通往光荣的道路总是艰难崎岖的。现在我就要到世界上去完成我的重大使命。"

这段路程非常辛苦，但比起后来所经受的种种折磨痛苦却又不算什么。黏土被抛进一个槽子里面，然后便是一番掺和、捶打、搅拌、践踏，真是不堪其苦。但是一想到某种美好崇高的事物必将从这一番痛苦中产生出来，也就感到释然了。黏土坚信，只要它能耐心地等待下去，总有一天它将得到重酬。

接着它被放到一只飞速转动着的转盘上去，自己也跟着旋转起来，那感觉真好像自己即将被甩得粉身碎骨。在旋转

new form.

Then an unknown hand put it into an oven, and fires were kindled about it — fierce and penetrating — hotter than all the heats of summer that had ever brooded upon the bank of the river. But through all, the clay held itself together and endured its trials[1], in the confidence of a great future. "Surely," it thought, "I am intended for something very splendid, since such pains are taken with me. Perhaps I am fashioned for the ornament of a temple, or a precious vase for the table of a king."

At last the baking was finished. The clay was taken from the furnace and set down upon a board, in the cool air, under the blue sky. The tribulation was passed. The reward was at hand.

Close beside the board there was a pool of water, not very deep, nor very clear, but calm enough to reflect, with impartial[2] truth, every image that fell upon it. There, for the first time, as it was lifted from the board, the clay saw its new shape, the reward of all its patience and pain, the consummation of its hopes — a common flower-pot, straight and stiff, red and ugly. And then it felt that it was not destined for a king's house, nor for a palace of art, because it was made without glory or beauty or honor; and it murmured

1 trial /'traɪəl/ n. 尝试，努力，试验
2 impartial /ɪm'pɑːʃl/ adj. 公平的，不偏不倚的

中，仿佛有一种神力把它紧紧捏在一起，在它经历了一切眩晕痛苦之后，觉得自己已经开始变成一种新的形状。

然后一只陌生的手把它放进炉灶，周围烈火熊熊 —— 真是痛心刺骨 —— 那灼热程度远比盛夏时节河边的艳阳要厉害得多。但整个期间，黏土始终十分坚强，经受了一切考验，对自己的伟大前途充满信心。它心想，"既然人家对我下了这么大的工夫，我是注定要有一番锦绣前程的。看来我不是去充当庙堂殿宇里的华美装饰，便是成为帝王几案上的名贵花瓶。"

最后烘焙完毕。黏土从灶中被取出，放在一块木板上面，让它在蓝天之下凉风之中去慢慢冷却。一番磨难既过，报偿的日子也就不远了。

木板之旁便有一泓潭水，水虽不很深也不很清，但却波纹平静，能把潭边的事物确切地反映出来。当黏土被人从板上拿起来时，它才第一次窥见了自己新的形状，而这便是它千辛万苦之后的报偿，它的全部心愿的成果 —— 一只普普通通的花盆，线条粗硬，又红又丑。这时它才感觉到自己既不可能登帝王之家，也不可能入艺术之宫，因为自己

against the unknown maker, saying, "Why hast thou made me thus?"

Many days it passed in sullen discontent. Then it was filled with earth, and something — it knew not what — but something rough and brown and dead-looking, was thrust into the middle of the earth and covered over. The clay rebelled[1] at this new disgrace. "This is the worst of all that has happened to me, to be filled with dirt and rubbish. Surely I am a failure."

But presently it was set in a greenhouse, where the sunlight fell warm upon it, and water was sprinkled over it, and day by day as it waited, a change began to come to it. Something was stirring within it — a new hope. Still it was ignorant, and knew not what the new hope meant.

One day the clay was lifted again from its place, and carried into a great church. Its dream was coming true after all. It had a fine part to play in the world. Glorious music flowed over it. It was surrounded with flowers. Still it could not understand. So it whispered to another vessel of clay, like itself, close beside it, "Why have they set me here? Why do all the people look toward us?" And the other vessel answered, "Do you not know? You are carrying a royal scepter of lilies. Their petals are white as snow, and the heart of them is like pure

---

1 rebel /rɪˈbel/ v. 反抗，谋反，抵抗

的外貌一点也不高雅华贵；于是它对自己那位无名的制造者喃喃抱怨起来，"你为什么把我造成这等模样？"

自此一连数日它都抑郁不快。接着它被装上了土，另外还有一件东西 —— 是什么它弄不清，但灰黄粗糙，样子难看 —— 也被插到了土的中间，然后被盖上。这个新的屈辱引起了黏土的极大不满。"我的不幸现在到了极点，让人装起脏土垃圾来了。我这一生算是完了。"

但是过了不久，黏土又被放进了一间温室，这里阳光和煦地照射着它，并且有人经常给它喷水，这样就在它一天天静静等候的时候，某种变化终于开始到来。某种东西正在体内萌动 —— 莫非是希望重生！但它对此仍然毫不理解，也不懂得这个希望意味着什么。

有一天，黏土又被人从原地搬起，送进一座宏伟的教堂。它多年的梦想这次终于可以实现了。它在世界上的确是有所作为的。这时空际仙乐阵阵，周围百花飘香。但它仍然不明白这一切。于是它就向旁边和它一模一样的另一个黏土器皿悄声问道："为什么我被他们放在这里？为什么所有的

gold. The people look this way because the flower is the most wonderful in the world. And the root of it is in your heart."

Then the clay was content, and silently thanked its maker, because, though an earthen vessel, it held so great a treasure.

人都向我们凝望？"那个器皿答道："怎么你还不知道吗？你身上现在载员着一株状如王杖的美丽百合。它的花瓣皎白如雪，它的花心如同灿烂纯金。人们的目光之所以都集中到这里，是因为这株花乃是世界上最了不起的，而花的根就在你的心里。"

这时黏土心满意足了，它暗暗地感谢它的制造者，因为虽然自己只是一只泥土器皿，但里面装的却是一件稀世奇珍。

含英咀华

本文是一篇寓言故事。作者以流畅的文笔叙述了一撮黏土经过各种考验，终于在平凡的生涯中，发挥了不平常的作用，寓意深刻。让我们想到自己的人生，只要一直坚持自己的信念，永不放弃，最后一定会实现梦想。

Skye Thomas
斯凯·托马斯

斯凯·托马斯，美国的自由撰稿人，也是网站"明日边缘"（*www.TomorrowsEdge. net*）的首席执行官。她出版了五本书，其大多数文章都是励志作品，而且都可以从她的"明日边缘"网站中读到。

What If I Fall Flat on My Face?

I know what you are thinking. "What if I fall flat on my face?" I hope you do. Sounds awful, I know, but I really think the best thing that can happen to you is for you to take a timid little leap[1] and fall flat on your face. Then, I want to see you get back up, evaluate what you did wrong, and jump again, keep on taking that leap of faith and learn from each and every mistake until you become used to jumping and used to falling. Then, you will get over the fear of falling and you will finally begin to concentrate on flying. I want to see you run with everything you have and dive into your dreams with so much passion and fire that you forget all about the possibility of failing. You will never find your wings until you do.

The fear of failure is a cruel and stupid trick we pull on ourselves. The fact that the fear of failure stops us from going after our goals and dreams means that we have already failed. I ask you this, who cares if you fail? Brilliant people fail every single day. Brave tenacious[2] people fall flat on their faces and even get laughed at every single day. Here's an example

---

1 leap /liːp/ *n.* 跳跃，剧增，急变
2 tenacious /təˈneɪʃəs/ *adj.* 顽强的；紧握的

假如一败涂地，我将如何自处？

我知道你在琢磨什么，"如果我一跤摔倒，一败涂地，那可如何是好？"我倒希望你跌倒。听上去不是个滋味，这我知道，但是，我确实认为，在你生活中发生的最美妙的事情，莫过于小心翼翼向前跃出一小步，结果却脸朝地摔个正着。接下来，我希望看到你爬起来，想想哪里出了差错，然后再继续向前跃进。持之以恒，满怀信念，继续向前跃进，从每个失误中汲取教训，直到你对跃进和跌跤均习以为常。你将自然而然地摆脱对摔跤的恐惧，开始全神贯注，怀着似火的激情进入你的梦想世界，将失败的可能性置之度外，除此之外便不可能找到你梦想的翅膀。

对失败忐忑不安，是我们对自己残酷而愚蠢的捉弄。倘若担心失败而放弃追求自己的目标和梦想，那就意味着我们已经失败了。我问你，假如你失败了，谁会在乎？才华横溢的人每天都会遭遇失败。无所

of a perfectly nice person who has been known to fail, Christopher Reeve[1]. How many mornings did he wake up telling himself that he was going to walk and then went to bed having failed yet again. Great guy, people love him. He's not going to let a little thing like yesterday's failure stop him from working hard again today. He's an inspiration to everyone who knows him. Who ever planted that stupid idea in our heads that we had to be successful at every single thing every single day in order to be likeable?

What is failure anyway? In my eyes, Christopher Reeve is definitely not a failure. Nobody with that much tenacity[2], focus, and drive is failing. He is a real hero. You haven't failed until you have given up trying. As long as you are still taking leaps of faith, you're still a winner. Failure, like everything else, has its breaking point. At some point, if you hit at it in the same spot over and over again it eventually breaks. How many light bulbs[3] did Thomas Edison make before he got it right? Most people don't know the answer to that because they don't care how many times he failed before he finally succeeded. He kept learning from each attempt, adapting to the new information, stayed the course, held the

---

1 **Christopher Reeve:** 克里斯托夫·里夫（1952~2004），因成功塑造"超人"形象而被人们永远铭记。1995年，他不幸因堕马而瘫痪，一度心情颓废，甚至考虑过自杀，但在妻子的支持下，终于重树信心，激发了与病魔斗争的勇气，并创建了瘫痪研究中心以及设立了里夫瘫痪基金
2 **tenacity** /təˈnæsəti/　*n.* 顽强意志
3 **bulb** /bʌlb/　*n.* 电灯泡，球状物

畏惧、不屈不挠的人每天都会摔倒在地，甚至饱受他人的嘲笑挖苦。例如，众所周知的克里斯托夫·里夫每天都要体味失败的滋味。有多少个清晨，他醒来告诉自己他能够行走自如，到了夜幕降临就寝时，却发现自己再度遭受失败。他是伟大的，人们都敬爱他。一件不足挂齿的小事，诸如昨日的失败，绝对不会阻止他今天的再次努力。他令所有知道他的人深受鼓舞。如果要招人喜欢，我们就必须每天让每件事都成功，是谁将这个愚蠢的念头灌输到我们头脑中的？

那么，什么是失败呢？在我眼中，克里斯托夫·里夫绝对不是失败的人。那样有毅力、有目标、有闯劲的人不会失败。他是真正的英雄好汉。只要不放弃努力尝试，你就还没有失败。只要仍然有信心勇往直前，你就是胜利者。如同其他任何事情一样，失败有一个突破点。只要你一次又一次地击打同一个突破点，到了一定程度你终将击破失败。在成功之前，托马斯·爱迪生制作了多少个电灯泡？很多人对这个问题一无所知，因为他们对爱迪生终获成功之前经了多少

dream, and didn't let the fear of failure nor the fear of other people's ridicule[1] stop him.

One of the reasons that I think we hear so many stories of immigrants coming to this country and making it big is because they were raised on stories of the ability to create whatever kind of life you envision[2] for yourself here. It's like all the stories they grew hearing about how everyone has the right to succeed in America overriding[3] any underlying belief that they themselves could fail. They don't have a fear of failure so they just roll up their sleeves and get to work making their dreams come true. Sure they stumble[4] and fall and learn a few lessons along the way, but they certainly don't give up and quit.

Afraid of what other people are going to think of you if you fail? Have you ever met someone who played it ultra[5] safe that was very impressive? People who don't take risks are seldom if ever cheered, admired, or in the limelight[6]. Besides, Americans love an underdog[7]. We love to see some scrappy[8] go-getter who has no business thinking they can win. We love to watch that same person stumble and fall a few times only to pick themselves up and really make something of themselves. It's the American

1 ridicule /'rɪdɪkjuːl/ n. 嘲笑，愚弄，笑柄
2 envision /ɪn'vɪʒn/ v. 预想
3 override /ˌəʊvəˈraɪd/ v. 拒绝，藐视
4 stumble /'stʌmb(ə)l/ v. 跌跌撞撞地走；蹒跚而行
5 ultra /'ʌltrə/ adj. 过度的，过激的，极端的
6 limelight /'laɪmlaɪt/ n. 公众注意的中心
7 underdog /'ʌndədɒg/ n. 处于劣势的人；弱者
8 scrappy /'skræpi/ adj. 斗志旺盛的

次失败漠不关心。爱迪生不断从每次失败中学习，不断适应新的情况，不懈努力，坚持梦想，不让对失败的恐惧和别人的冷嘲热讽阻止他前进的脚步。

我们听到过许多来到这个国家并获得辉煌成功的移民的故事。我认为原因之一是他们从小便听说在这里能够创造自己所想要的生活。他们在成长过程中听到过各式各样的故事，说在美国每个人都有权追求成功，所有这些都有利于让他们克服自己可能失败的潜意识，让他们对失败毫无惧色。因此他们只是卷起衣袖，开始奋斗，去实现理想。当然，他们将会在人生的旅途上磕磕碰碰，摔跤跌倒，并不断吸取经验教训，但是他们永远不会轻言放弃。

如果失败，你会为别人将如何看待你而忧心忡忡吗？你是否曾经遇到过既求万无一失又令你难忘的人？不冒风险，就很难获得人们的喝彩、敬佩或瞩目。另外，美国人对失败者心存宽容，我们喜爱看到一些斗志旺盛、有进取心的人，他们对输赢不作考虑。我们希望看到这样的人跌跌撞撞

Dream. Hollywood knows it. They have made an entire industry of showing us the stories of underdogs who dust themselves off and finally become winners. Nobody pays money to watch a movie about some perfect person who designs a perfect dream and experiences, a flawless life while accomplishing everything they set out to do easily and effortlessly. Boooooooring! We don't like people who come across as too perfect anyway. So go ahead and fail, it gives us a reason to pay attention to you, to relate to you, to cheer you on.

One of the best pieces of advice I was ever given on this subject was back in high school when I was first learning how to water-ski. I was told "if you aren't falling down, then you aren't trying very hard. You are playing it safely, staying in your comfort zone. You aren't getting any better." That pushed me to get past my fear of falling. I beat the heck out of my poor body that summer, but I also made impressive gains in my ability to master the sport. Nobody talked about how many times I fell that summer nor how black and blue I was, they only talked about how fast I was learning and what a great job I was doing. My teacher would sit back with this self-satisfied smirk[1] on his face because only he knew how hard it had been for me to push past that comfort zone to allow myself permission to fall down. Nothing beats taking

---

1 smirk /smɜːk/   *n.*   得意的笑

摔倒在地，最终翻身而起，反败为胜。这就是美国梦。好莱坞深谙此道，它不断向我们展示郁郁不得志的人掸尽身上的灰尘，最终成功的种种故事。没有人愿意掏钱去看一部讲述一个完美的人设计了一个完美的梦想，轻而易举地完成他计划的事情，并经历了一个完美人生的电影。这将令人厌烦不堪。不管怎么说，我们就是不喜欢尽善尽美的人，因此只管奋勇向前去经历失败，这至少给了我们一个理由去关注你、与你交往、给你鼓励。

关于这一问题，我曾得到的金玉良言之一还是在中学时代获得的。那时我刚刚开始练习滑水橇。我被告知："如果不摔倒，那么就是你努力不够。你是在力求稳妥，停留在安全区内，这样你不会有任何进步。"这些话激励我克服了对摔倒的恐惧。那年夏天，我的身体伤痕累累，但是在这一项目上我取得了突飞猛进的成绩。没有人谈起那个夏天我摔倒了多少次或是我怎样被摔得遍体鳞伤，他们只是谈论我学得有多快，我做得有多棒。我的老师坐在后面，满意地笑着，因为只有他了解我为了突

that big bite out of life and having it bite back just a bit! Laugh it off and dive in again.

Are you really going to shelve[1] something so dear to your heart because you might fail? If I could promise you that you had only fail twice and on the third attempt you would succeed, then would you go ahead and suffer through the first two failures in order to get to that third time? Of course, you would. All that's left to debate is how many times. So go ahead ... take that first leap of faith.

破安全区，不畏惧摔倒而付出了多少。向生活勇敢挑战，并遭遇些许挫折，没有比这更刺激的了！对这些挫折一笑置之，然后继续前行。

难道你真的因为可能失败，就打算将自己心中的珍宝束之高阁吗？假如我可以向你保证你将只会失败两次，在第三次尝试时你将成功，那么你会不会为了达到第三次而勇敢向前，经历前两次失败的痛苦呢？你肯定会。剩下要讨论的问题就是到底需要经历多少次失败了。那么行动起来吧……满怀信心地迈出你的第一步。

---

1 shelve /ʃelv/　v.　搁置

不经一番寒彻骨 怎得梅花扑鼻香

含英咀华

　　本文摘自托马斯的《超越内心批评》(*Beyond the Inner Critic, 2004*)第一章。文章以十分积极的态度要读者相信，只要不放弃努力，就一直有成功的希望。而在努力的过程中，你可能面对失败，可不经历风雨怎么见彩虹？不体会失败，又怎能享受最后成功时的成就感呢？那就让我们为理想而奋斗，不管可能遭遇多少次失败，都勇敢地"行动起来吧，满怀信心地迈出你的第一步"。读过本文之后，也许你就会明白为什么断臂的维纳斯被称为爱与美的女神了。

Alice Meynell

Alice Meynell
艾丽斯·梅内尔

艾丽斯·梅内尔(1847~1922)，英国诗人、作家、妇女参政主义者，颇得王尔德（Oscar Wilde）的赏识。她的第一部诗集名为《序曲》(Preludes, 1875)。婚后的梅内尔虽然是八个孩子的母亲，但仍热衷于文学活动。她在丈夫的出版社进行编辑工作的同时，还坚持进行个人诗歌和散文创作。梅内尔还是西赛莉·汉密顿（Cicely Hamilton）创立的"女作家参政权联盟"（Women Writers' Suffrage League）的主要成员（该组织在1908到1919年间非常活跃）。

不经一番寒彻骨 怎得梅花扑鼻香

The Rhythm of Life

If life is not always poetical, it is at least metrical[1]. Periodicity[2] rules over the mental experience of man, according to the path of the orbit[3] of his thoughts. Distances are not gauged[4], ellipses not measured, velocities[5] not ascertained[6], times not known. Nevertheless, the recurrence is sure. What the mind suffered last week, or last year, it does not suffer now; but it will suffer again next week or next year. Happiness is not a matter of events; it depends upon the tides of the mind. Disease is metrical, closing in at shorter and shorter periods towards death, sweeping abroad at longer and longer intervals towards recovery. Sorrow for one cause was intolerable yesterday, and will be intolerable tomorrow; today it is easy to bear, but the cause has not passed. Even the burden of a spiritual distress unsolved is bound to leave the heart to a temporary peace; and remorse[7] itself does not remain — it returns. Gaiety[8] takes us by a dear surprise. If we had made a course of notes of its visits, we might have been on the watch, and would have had an

生活的节奏

假如生活不总是充满诗情画意，它至少是富有悠扬韵律的。从思想轨道的路径来看，人的内心体验呈现周期性。不知彼此距离有多远，不知椭圆轨道有多长，不知运行速度有多快，不知循环周期有多久。但是，周而复始的循环是确定无疑的。在过去的一周或一年中，内心曾经遭受的痛苦，现在已经烟消云散了；但接下来的一周或一年里，痛苦仍然会卷土重来。快乐不在于我们经历的是是非非，而取决于心灵的潮起潮落。疾病是带有节奏规律的，行将就木之际疾病来袭的周期愈来愈短，身体复原时疾病的发作周期愈来愈长。因为某事，痛不欲生，这种痛楚昨日曾不堪承受，明日也将不堪承受；今日却不难忍受，尽管伤心事并未过去。甚至困扰精神之重负也定会有让内心得到片刻安宁之时；悔恨本身并非驻足不去，它只不过是再度光临。快乐令人又惊又喜。倘若觉察到快乐来临的路线，我们可能会翘首以待，因此快

---

1 metrical /ˈmetrɪkl/ *adj.* 韵律的，有韵律的
2 periodicity /ˌpɪərɪˈɒdɪsəti/ *n.* 定期性，周期性，周期数
3 orbit /ˈɔːbɪt/ *n.* 轨道，人生道路
4 gauged /geɪdʒ/ *v.* 测量；判断
5 velocity /vəˈlɒsəti/ *n.* 速度，速率
6 ascertain /ˌæsəˈteɪn/ *v.* 确定，探知
7 remorse /rɪˈmɔːs/ *n.* 懊悔，悔恨
8 gaiety /ˈɡeɪəti/ *n.* 愉快，快活，高兴

expectation instead of a discovery. No one makes such observations; in all the diaries of students of the interior world, there have never come to light the records of the Kepler of such cycles. But Thomas à Kempis[1] knew of the recurrences, if he did not measure them. In his cell alone with the elements — "What wouldst thou more than these? for out of these were all things made" — he learnt the stay to be found in the depth of the hour of bitterness, and the remembrance that restrains the soul at the coming of the moment of delight, giving it a more conscious welcome, but presaging[2] for it an inexorable[3] flight. And "rarely, rarely comest thou," sighed Shelley, not to delight merely, but to the spirit of delight. Delight can be compelled beforehand, called, and constrained[4] to our service — Ariel can be bound to a daily task; but such artificial violence throws life out of meter, and it is not the spirit that is thus compelled. That flits[5] upon an orbit elliptically[6] or parabolically[7] or hyperbolically[8] curved, keeping no man knows what trysts with time.

It seems fit that Shelley and the author of the *Imitation* should both have been keen and simple enough to perceive these flights, and

乐如期而至，而非突如其来。无人做过这种观察；在人们关于内心世界的所有日记中，尚未出现开普勒式的人物记录过这种循环往复。但是坎普滕的托马斯知道这种循环，尽管他并未测量它的周期。——"除此之外，夫复何求？万事万物皆由此构成"——他发现在悲伤回顾之时反能找到快乐的逗留。快乐时刻来临之时，人的心灵因过去的记忆而不致放纵无忌，从而体会快乐之情更深刻，并预感其会转瞬即逝，难以长留。"你甚少，甚少光临"，雪莱长吁短叹，伤感的并非快乐本身，而是快乐的精灵。我们可以事先强迫快乐听候我们随意调遣，伺候我们——每日分派埃里厄尔任务；但是这种人为的勉强破坏了生活的节奏韵律，何况强迫并非快乐的精灵。快乐的精灵在椭圆形、抛物线形或双曲线形的轨道上飞来飞去，无人知晓他与时间有怎样的约会。

雪莱与《效法基督》的作者可以敏锐而简单地察觉到快乐精灵的飞翔往来，并猜测其周期性，这并非巧合。这两个人的灵魂与他们生活的多个世界中的精灵密切接触，因此任

---

1 Thomas à Kempis: 托马斯·肯皮斯（1380~1471），原名 Thomas Hemerken，德国修士及神学家。1387年进入阿格尼滕伯格的奥古斯丁修道院，1413年接受神职，其后终身从事抄写书稿和辅导新修士的工作。据说他就是继《圣经》以后基督教文学史上最具影响力的信仰著作《效法基督》的作者。该书文词朴实无华，强调精神生活高于物质生活，并确信以基督为中心必得善报

2 presage /'presɪdʒ/ v. 预兆，预示，预言

3 inexorable /ɪn'eksərəbl/ adj. 不为所动的，坚决不变的

4 constrain /kən'streɪn/ v. 强迫，勉强，驱使

5 flit /flɪt/ v. 掠过

6 elliptically /ɪ'lɪptɪkli/ adv. 椭圆形地，省略地

7 parabolically /ˌpærə'bɒlɪk(ə)li/ adv. 抛物线地；用比喻说明地

8 hyperbolically /ˌhaɪpə'bɒlɪkli/ adv. 双曲线地

to guess at the order of this periodicity. Both souls were in close touch with the spirits of their several worlds, and no deliberate human rules, no infractions of the liberty and law of the universal movement, kept from them the knowledge of recurrences. Eppur simuove. They knew that presence does not exist without absence; they knew that what is just upon its flight of farewell is already on its long path of return. They knew that what is approaching to the very touch is hastening towards departure. 'O wind,' cried Shelley, in autumn,

'O wind,

If winter comes, can spring be far behind?'

They knew that the flux is equal to the reflux; that to interrupt with unlawful recurrences, out of time, is to weaken the impulse of onset and retreat; the sweep and impetus of movement. To live in constant efforts after an equal life, whether the equality be sought in mental production, or in spiritual sweetness, or in the joy of the senses, is to live without either rest or full activity. The souls of certain of the saints, being singularly simple and single, have been in the most complete subjection to the law of periodicity. Ecstasy and desolation visited them by seasons. They endured, during spaces of vacant time, the interior loss of all for which they had sacrificed the world. They rejoiced in the uncovenanted[1] beatitude[2] of sweetness alighting

1 uncovenanted /ʌnˈkʌv(ə)nəntɪd/ adj. 盟约（尤指上帝与人所立之约）中未规定（或保证、认可）的，不受盟约（或条约）约束的
2 beatitude /bɪˈætɪtjuːd/ n. 至福，祝福

何人类的繁文缛节，任何对普遍运动的自由和规则的违背，都不能阻止他们发现这一周而复始的规律。"它仍然在转动。"他们知道没有暂离便没有来临；他们知道飘然离去意味着漫长的回程；他们知道姗姗来迟、似乎触手可及的东西却又正急忙转身匆匆而去。"啊！风，"雪莱在秋季感慨万端，

"啊！风，

如果冬天来了，春天还会远吗？"

他们知道潮涨意味着潮落，不合时宜的、人为的周期干扰将使潮流的进退失据，削弱运动的气势和原动力。如果一生矢志追求平等的生活，无论是在智力产出上的平等、在精神惬意上的平等抑或是在感官享受上的平等，生活都将毫无安宁，也了无生气。一些圣人的生活单纯专一，与众不同，他们的灵魂完全符合周期性的规律。欣喜与忧伤在他们身上交替发生。在头脑空虚的时候，他们忍受着种种放弃凡尘俗世的内心痛苦。为了心中点亮的不受拘束的甜美祝福，他们欣喜不已。诗人骚客与他们一样，在漫漫的人生旅途中，缪斯女神有三次或十次降临到他们身边，抚摸他们，又抛弃他们。然

in their hearts. Like them are the poets whom, three times or ten times in the course of a long life, the Muse has approached, touched, and forsaken. And yet hardly like them; not always so docile, nor so wholly prepared for the departure, the brevity, of the golden and irrevocable[1] hour. Few poets have fully recognized the metrical absence of their Muse. For full recognition is expressed in one only way — silence.

It has been found that several tribes in Africa and in America worship the moon, and not the sun; a great number worship both; but no tribes are known to adore the sun, and not the moon. For the periodicity of the sun is still in part a secret; but that of the moon is modestly apparent, perpetually influential. On her depend the tides; and she is Selene, mother of Herse, bringer of the dews that recurrently irrigate lands where rain is rare. More than any other companion of earth is she the measurer. Early Indo-Germanic languages knew her by that name. Her metrical phases are the symbol of the order of recurrence. Constancy in approach and in departure is the reason of her inconstancies. Juliet will not receive a vow spoken in invocation of the moon; but Juliet did not live to know that love itself has tidal times — lapses and ebbs which are due to the metrical rule of the interior heart, but which the lover vainly and unkindly attributes to some outward alteration in the beloved. For

而，两者迥然而异的是，诗人并不总是驯服的，因此也不会为与宝贵而不可改变的时光的离去和小别做好充分的准备。对于他们的缪斯离开的规律，很少有诗人能够充分认识到。因为对此的充分认识仅有一种方式，那就是沉默。

在非洲和美洲的一些部落，人们不是膜拜太阳，而是膜拜月亮；很多部落则两者都膜拜；没有哪支部落只膜拜太阳，不膜拜月亮。因为太阳的运动规律还有一部分不为人知，而月亮的周期规律却很显著，无时不感到其威力。月亮决定着潮汐的涨落；她是塞勒涅，是赫斯之母；在降雨稀少的地方，她带来露水滋润大地。同地球的其他卫星相比，月亮是度量者。早期的印欧语就是这样称呼月亮的。她度量的方式就是其阴晴圆缺的象征。恒久不变地靠近和远离，正是她变化的原因所在。朱丽叶不接受指月盟誓，但她不知道爱情本身也是有起有落的——爱的消长是由内心的反复规律所决定的，但是恋人徒劳而无情地归咎于他的爱人外表的某些变化。因为除了非同一般的人之外，人是很难有周

1 irrevocable /ɪˈrevəkəbl/   adj.   不能唤回的，不能取消的，不能变更的

man — except those elect already named — is hardly aware of periodicity. The individual man either never learns it fully, or learns it late. And he learns it so late, because it is a matter of cumulative[1] experience upon which cumulative evidence is lacking. It is in the after-part of each life that the law is learnt so definitely as to do away with the hope or fear of continuance. That young sorrow comes so near to despair is a result of this young ignorance. So is the early hope of great achievement. Life seems so long, and its capacity so great, to one who knows nothing of all the intervals it needs must hold — intervals between aspirations, between actions, pauses as inevitable as the pauses of sleep. And life looks impossible to the young unfortunate, unaware of the inevitable and unfailing refreshment. It would be for their peace to learn that there is a tide in the affairs of men, in a sense more subtle — if it is not too audacious[2] to add a meaning to Shakespeare — than the phrase was meant to contain. Their joy is flying away from them on its way home; their life will wax and wane[3]; and if they would be wise, they must wake and rest in its phases, knowing that they are ruled by the law that commands all things — a sun's revolutions and the rhythmic pangs[4] of maternity.

---

1 cumulative /ˈkjuːmjələtɪv/ *adj.* 累积的
2 audacious /ɔːˈdeɪʃəs/ *adj.* 大胆的，放肆的
3 wax and wane 盈亏（盛衰）。例如：**Throughout history empires have waxed and waned.** （历史上各个帝国革故鼎新均有兴衰。）
4 pang /pæŋ/ *n.* 剧痛，悲痛，苦闷

期意识的。一个人要么对此永远浑然不知，要么认识到时，为时已晚。他之所以很晚才懂得这点，是因为这是一个缺乏积累证据基础上的经验积累。一个人直至其后半生，才能清楚地明白月亮阴晴圆缺的规律，不再因此而期冀殷殷或忧心忡忡。年轻人对这一规律的无知，导致了他们产生濒临绝望的痛苦。成就非凡事业的期望也是如此。人生漫长，潜力无穷。对于那些对人生的周期循环毫无所知的人来说，这些间隔——愿望与渴望的间隔、行动与行动的间隔——如同睡眠的间隔一样，是不可避免的。对间隔的不可避免与无穷无尽的无知，使得人生对时运不济的年轻人来说，似乎是不可思议。他们应该明白，人间世事如同潮汐一般有涨有落——倘若我这不算大胆的揣测莎翁的本意——它应当包含这层意思。快乐从他们的身上离去，走上回家的路；他们的生命也会有月盈月亏，如果他们明智的话，他们就必须顺从这一规律，知道这一规律能掌控世间的万事万物——这包括太阳的旋转甚至于产妇的阵痛。

不经一番寒彻骨 怎得梅花扑鼻香

含英咀华

本文以一个女性所特有的洞察力探讨了人们内心体验的周期性，说明了人生的节奏韵律。特别是时运不济的人，更应该了解这种周期性，把握生命的节奏，不要让一时的烦恼影响自己。因为人生悲喜交织、世事起伏犹如潮起潮落，人生既然有低谷，自然就会有高潮。

Theodore Roosevelt
西奥多·罗斯福

西奥多·罗斯福（1858~1919），美国军事家、政治家，第二十六任总统。在其任期内，制定资源保护政策，保护了许多国有森林、矿产、石油等资源，因此受到美国人民的爱戴。

The Strenuous[1] Life

艰辛的人生

A life of slothful[2] ease, a life of that peace which springs merely from lack either of desire or of power to strive[3] after great things, is as little worthy of a nation as of an individual. ... We do not admire the man of timid peace. We admire the man who embodies victorious efforts, the man who never wrongs[4] his neighbor, who is prompt to help a friend, but who has those virile[5] qualities necessary to win in the stern[6] strife[7] of actual life. It is hard to fail, but it is worse never to have tried to succeed. In this life we get nothing save by effort. Freedom from effort in the present merely means that there has been effort stored up in the past. A man can be freed from the necessity of work only by the fact that he or his fathers before him have worked to good purpose. If the freedom thus purchased is used aright[8], and the man still does actual work, though of a different kind, whether as a writer or a general, whether in the field of politics or in the field of exploration and adventure, he shows he deserves his good fortune.

一种怠惰安逸的生活，一种仅仅是由于缺少追寻伟大事物的渴望或能力而导致的悠闲生活，这无论对国家还是个人都是毫无价值的。…… 我们不欣赏那种怯懦安逸的人。我们钦佩那种表现出奋发图强精神的人，那种从不屈待邻人，能随时帮助朋友，但是也具有那些刚健的品质，足以在现实生活的严酷斗争中获取胜利的人。失败是难以忍受的，但更为糟糕的是从来不努力去争取成功。在人的这一生中，任何收获都要通过努力去得到。目前不作任何的努力，只不过意味着在过去储着了努力。一个人不必工作，除非他或其先辈们曾经努力工作过，并取得了丰厚的收获。倘若他能把获得的这种自由加以正确地运用，仍然做些实际的工作，尽管那些工作是属于另一类的，不论是做一名作家还是将军，不论是在政界还是在探险和冒险方面做些事情，都表明了他没有辜负自己的好运。

1 strenuous /'strenjuəs/　adj.　艰苦的；奋力的
2 slothful /'sləʊθfl/　adj.　怠惰的，懒惰的
3 strive /straɪv/　v.　(strove, striven; strived, strived) 努力，奋斗，力争
4 wrong /rɒŋ/　v.　不公正对待
5 virile /'vɪraɪl/　adj.　有男子气概的；精力充沛的
6 stern /stɜːn/　adj　严厉的，坚决的，可怖的
7 strife /straɪf/　n.　争吵
8 aright /ə'raɪt/　adv.　正确地

But if he treats this period of freedom from the need of actual labor as a period, not of preparation, but of mere enjoyment, even though perhaps not of vicious[1] enjoyment, he shows that he is simply a cumberer[2] on the earth's surface; and he surely unfits himself to hold his own place with his fellows, if the need to do so should again arise. A mere life of ease is not in the end a very satisfactory life, and, above all, it is a life which ultimately unfits those who follow it for serious work in the world.

As it is with the individual, so it is with the nation. It is a base untruth to say that happy is the nation that has no history. Thrice[3] happy is the nation that has a glorious history. Far better it is to dare mighty things, to win glorious triumphs, even though checkered by failure, than to take rank with those poor spirits who neither enjoy much nor suffer much, because they live in the gray twilight that knows neither victory nor defeat.

然而，尚若他未将这段需要从事实际工作的自由时期用于准备，而仅仅是用于享乐——即使他所从事的或许并非不良的享乐——那也表明他只是地球表面上的一个累赘；而且如果那种需要再度出现的话，他肯定无法在同僚之中维持自己的地位。一种纯粹安逸的生活终究并不是一种很令人满意的生活，而且，最重要的是，过那种生活的人最终肯定没有能力担当起世上之重任。

对于个人是如此，对于国家也是这样。有人说一个没有历史的国家是得天独厚的，这是根本错误的。一种得天独厚的优越感来源于一个国家所具有的光荣历史。 敢于向强有力的事物挑战，去夺取辉煌的胜利，即使遭受挫折也比苟且偷安强得多，因为得过且过的人生活在暗淡的暮光之中，既体验不到胜利的欢乐，也尝试不到失败的痛苦。

不经一番寒彻骨 怎得梅花扑鼻香

---

1 vicious /'vɪʃəs/ adj. 恶毒的，凶残的；剧烈的，严重的
2 cumberer /'kʌmbərə/ n. 拖累
3 thrice /θraɪs/ adv. 三倍；三次

含英咀华

本文节选自《赞奋斗不息》(*In Praise of the Strenuous Life*)，是1899年4月10日西奥多·罗斯福在芝加哥为纪念内战结束三十四周年做的演讲。文章中，他告诉人们要"向强有力的事物挑战，去夺取辉煌的胜利，即使遭受挫折也比苟且偷安强得多，因为得过且过的人生活在暗淡的暮光之中，既体验不到胜利的欢乐，也尝试不到失败的痛苦。"

Steve Porter

史蒂夫·波特

史蒂夫·波特 (1963~)，英格兰作家、学者和语言学家。其大部分作品是自己的经历和对生活的感悟，文笔朴实无华，风格清新隽永。

The 50-Percent Theory of Life

生活对半理论

I believe in the 50-percent theory. Half the time things are better than normal; the other half, they are worse. I believe life is a pendulum[1] swing. It takes time and experience to understand what normal is, and that gives me the perspective to deal with the surprises of the future.

Let's benchmark[2] the parameters: yes, I will die. I've dealt with the deaths of both parents, a best friend, a beloved boss and cherished pets. Some of these deaths have been violent, before my eyes, or slow and agonizing. Bad stuff, and it belongs at the bottom of the scale.

Then there are those high points: romance and marriage to the right person; having a child and doing those dad things like coaching my son's baseball team, paddling around the creek in the boat while he's swimming with the dogs, discovering his compassion so deep it manifests even in his kindness to snails, his imagination so vivid he builds a spaceship from a scattered pile of Legos[3].

But there is a vast meadow of life in the middle, where the bad and the good flip-flop

我信奉对半理论。生活时而无比顺畅，时而倒霉透顶。我觉得生活就像来回摆的钟摆。读懂生活的常态需要时间和阅历，而这也教会了我如何面对未来的意外。

让我们权衡一下生活中吉凶福祸：是的，我注定会死去。我已经经历了双亲，一位好友，一位敬爱的老板和心爱的宠物的死亡。有些突如其来，近在眼前，有些却缓慢痛苦。这些都是糟糕的事情，它们属于最坏的部分。

生活中也不乏高潮：坠入爱河缔结良缘；身为人父养育幼子，诸如指导儿子的棒球队，当他和狗嬉戏时摇桨划船，感受他如此强烈的同情心——即使对蜗牛也善待有加，发现他有如此丰富的想象力——即使用零散的乐高玩具积木也能堆出太空飞船。

但在生活最好与最坏部分之间有一片巨大的中间地带，其间各种好事坏事像杂技一样上下翻滚，轮番出现。这就

---

1 pendulum /'pendjələm/ n. 摆，钟摆
2 benchmark /'ben(t)ʃmɑːk/ v. 评估；衡量
3 Lego n. 为一种流行的垒高拼装玩具商标名称，此处指
      代这种玩具

acrobatically[1]. This is what convinces me to believe in the 50-percent theory.

One spring I planted corn too early in a bottomland so flood-prone that neighbors laughed. I felt chagrined[2] at the wasted effort. Summer turned brutal[3] — the worst heat wave and draught in my lifetime. The air conditioner died; the well went dry; the marriage ended; the job lost; the money gone. I was living lyrics from a country tune-music I loathed. Only a surging Kansas City Royals team buoyed[4] my spirits.

Looking back on that horrible summer, I soon understood that all succeeding good things merely offset[5] the bad. Worse than normal wouldn't last long. I am owed and savor the halcyon[6] times. They reinvigorate[7] me for the next nasty surprise and offer assurance[8] that I can thrive. The 50-percent theory even helps me see hope beyond my Royals' recent slump, a field of struggling rookies sown so that some years soon we can reap an October harvest.

For that one blistering summer, the ground moisture was just right, planting early allowed pollination[9] before heat withered the tops, and lack of rain spared the standing corn from floods.

1 acrobatically /ˌækrəˈbætɪkli/   adv.   杂技的
2 chagrined /ʃæˈɡrɪnd/   adj.   失望的，灰心的
3 brutal /ˈbruːtl/   adj.   野蛮的
4 buoy /bɔɪ/   v.   鼓舞；鼓励
5 offset /ˈɒfset/   v.   弥补，抵消
6 halcyon /ˈhælsɪən/   adj.   宁静的，平稳的
7 reinvigorate /ˌriːɪnˈvɪɡəreɪt/   v.   使再振作，使复生
8 assurance /əˈʃʊərəns/   n.   保证，确信
9 pollination /ˌpɒlɪˈneɪʃn/   n.   授粉

是让我信服对半理论的原因。

有一年春天，我在一块洼地上过早地种上了玉米。那块地极易遭到水淹，所以邻居们都嘲笑我。我为浪费了精力而感到懊恼。没想到夏天更为残酷——我经历了最糟糕的热浪和干旱。空调坏了，井干了，婚姻破裂了，工作丢了，钱也没了。我正经历着某首乡村歌曲中描绘的情节，我讨厌这种音乐。只有充满活力的堪萨斯皇家棒球队能鼓舞我的精神。

回首那个糟糕的夏天，我很快就明白了，所有后来出现的好事只不过是与坏事相互抵消。比较糟糕的境遇不会延宕过久；而太平时光是我应得的，我要尽情享受。它们为我注入活力以应对下一个险情，并确保我可以兴旺发达。对半理论甚至帮助我在堪萨斯皇家棒球队最近的低潮中看到希望——这是一块艰难行进的新手们耕耘的土地，只要播种了，几年之后我们就可以收获十月的金秋。

那个夏天天气酷热，地表湿度适宜，提早播种就可以在热浪打蔫顶部之前完成授粉，由于干旱更没有暴发洪水，田里的玉米得以保存。因此那个

That winter my crib overflowed with corn — fat, healthy three-to-a-stalk ears filled with kernels[1] from heel to tip—while my neighbors' fields yielded only brown, empty husks.

Although plantings past may have fallen below the 50-percent expectation, and they probably will again in the future, I am still sustained by the crop that flourishes during the drought.

冬天我的粮仓堆满了玉米——丰满、健康、一颗三穗且从头到脚都是饱满的玉米粒的玉米——而我的邻居们收获的只是晒黑的空壳。

尽管过去的播种可能没有达到百分之五十的收获期望，而且将来也可能是这样，但我仍然能靠着在旱季繁茂生长的庄稼而生存下去。

---

1 kernel /ˈkɜːnl/　*n.* 核心，中心，精髓

含英咀华

生活中，我们总是抱怨为什么别人总是万事如意，好运连连，为什么自己总是万分不幸，连连碰壁。其实命运是公平的，正如一句名言中说的，当上帝为你关上了一扇门，他就会为你开启一扇窗。正如本文作者所述，生活最好与最坏部分之间有一片巨大的中间地带，其间各种好事坏事像耍杂技一样上下翻滚，轮番出现。在文中，作者时而叙事，时而评论，让我们在平凡琐事中感受生活的真谛，真可谓是"一花一世界，一叶一菩提"。